P9-EEF-351

Set design by Vicki Mortimer *Photo by Joan Marcus*

Rupert Graves and Natasha Richardson in a scene from the New York production of *Closer.*

BY
PATRICK MARBER

★

★

DRAMATISTS
PLAY SERVICE
INC.

For Debra

ACKNOWLEDGMENTS

My grateful thanks to those mentioned elsewhere and also to:

Polly Draper, Dagmara Dominczyk, Joseph Murphy, Natacha Roi, J. Tucker Smith, Deirdre McCrane, John Barlow, Ilene Starger, Stuart Thompson, Sean Free, Kim Levin, Gene O'Donovan, Laura Brown MacKinnon, Ilona Somogyi, Rivka Katvan, Patsy Rodenburg, Traci Klainer, Janice Wilde, Kim Miscia, James Gardner, Sal Sclafani, Eric E. Smith, Christopher Cronin, James Michael Kabel, Kevin Mark Harris, Audrey Maher, Sonia Rivera, Mark Enright, Lisa Patterson, Lynn R. Camilo, Drew Hodges, Jim Edwards, Darby Lunceford, Joan Marcus, Adrian Bryan-Brown, John Cohen, Mark Roybal, Sherman Gross, Dennis Maher, Richard Beck, Kim Garnett, Terry McGarty, Carlos Jaramillo, Bobby Minor, Danny Paulos, Tim Barrett, David Macaaron, Ray Oravetz, John Payne, Paul Groothuis and Gerald Schoenfeld.

PM. London, August 1999.

AUTHOR'S NOTE

This revised version of *Closer* incorporates cuts, additions and rewrites effected in London and New York over the last two years. This version replaces those previously published and is the sole authorized version of the play.

An alternative "spoken" version of Scene 3 appears at the end of this text.

CLOSER was produced by Robert Fox, Scott Rudin, Roger Berlind, Carole Shorenstein Hays, ABC Inc., The Shubert Organization, and The Royal National Theatre on Broadway at the Music Box Theater on March 9, 1999. It was directed by Patrick Marber; the set design was by Vicki Mortimer; the lighting design was by Hugh Vanstone; the music was by Paddy Cunneen; the sound design was by Simon Baker; the Internet design was by John Owens; and the production stage manager was R. Wade Jackson. The cast was as follows:

ALICE.. Anna Friel
DAN .... Rupert Graves
LARRY .... Ciaran Hinds
ANNA.. Natasha Richardson

CLOSER was first presented in the Cottesloe auditorium of the Royal National Theatre (Richard Eyre, Artistic Director), London, England, on May 22, 1997. The cast was as follows:

ALICE.. Liza Walker
DAN .... Clive Owen
LARRY .... Ciaran Hinds
ANNA.. Sally Dexter

CHARACTERS

ALICE
A girl from the town.

DAN
A man from the suburbs.

LARRY
A man from the city.

ANNA
A woman from the country.

SETTING

The play is set in London in the 1990s.

Scene 1: January
Scene 2: June (The following year)
Scene 3: January (The following year)
Scene 4: January (The next day)
Scene 5: June (Five months later)
Scene 6: June (A year later)
Scene 7: September (Three months later)
Scene 8: October (A month later)
Scene 9: November (A month later)
Scene 10: December (A month later)
Scene 11: January (A month later)
Scene 12: July (Six months later)

The above dates are for information only. They should not be included in any production program or design.

All settings should be minimal.

CLOSER

ACT ONE

Scene 1

Hospital.

Early morning. (January.)

Alice is sitting. She is wearing a black coat. She has a rucksack by her side. Also, an old, brown, leather briefcase.

She rolls down one sock. She has a cut on her leg, quite bloody. She looks at it. She picks some strands of wool from the wound.

She looks at the briefcase. Thinks. Looks around. Opens it. She searches inside. She pulls out some sandwiches in silver foil. She looks at the contents, smiles, puts them back in the briefcase. Then she removes a green apple from the briefcase. She shines the apple and bites into it.

As she starts to chew Dan enters. He wears a suit and an overcoat. He stops, watches her eating his apple. He is holding two hot drinks in Styrofoam cups. After a while she sees him and smiles.

ALICE. Sorry. I was looking for a cigarette.
DAN. I've given up. *(He hands her a drink.)*

ALICE. Thanks. *(He checks his watch.)* Have you got to be somewhere?
DAN. Work. *(They sip their drinks.)* Didn't fancy my sandwiches?
ALICE. I don't eat fish.
DAN. Why not?
ALICE. Fish piss in the sea.
DAN. So do children.
ALICE. I don't eat children either. What's your work?
DAN. I'm a ... sort of journalist.
ALICE. What *sort?*
(Beat.)
DAN. I write obituaries.
(Beat.)
ALICE. Do you like it ... in the *dying* business?
DAN. It's a living.
ALICE. Did you grow up in a graveyard?
DAN. Yeah. Suburbia.
(Beat.)
ALICE. Do you think a doctor will come?
DAN. Eventually. Does it hurt?
ALICE. I'll live.
DAN. Shall I put your leg up?
ALICE. *Why?*
DAN. That's what people do in these situations.
ALICE. What is this "situation"? *(They look at each other.)*
DAN. Do you *want* me to put your leg up?
ALICE. Yes, please. *(Dan lifts her leg onto a chair.)*
DAN. I've got a mobile, is there anyone you'd like to phone?
ALICE. I don't know anyone.
Who cut off your crusts?
DAN. Me.
ALICE. Did your mother cut off your crusts when you were a little boy?
DAN. I believe she did, yes.
ALICE. You should eat your crusts.
DAN. You should stop smoking.
(Beat.)
ALICE. Thank you for scraping me off the road.

DAN. My pleasure.

ALICE. You *knight. (Dan looks at her.)*

DAN. You *damsel.*

Why didn't you look?

ALICE. I never look where I'm going.

DAN. We stood at the lights, I looked into your eyes and then you ... stepped into the road.

ALICE. Then what?

DAN. You were lying on the ground, you focused on me, you said, "Hallo, stranger."

ALICE. What a slut.

DAN. I noticed your leg was cut.

ALICE. Did you notice my *legs?*

DAN. Quite possibly.

ALICE. Then what?

DAN. The cabbie got out. He crossed himself. He said, "Thank fuck, I thought I'd killed her."

I said, "Let's get her to a hospital." He hesitated ... (I think he thought there'd be paperwork and he'd be held "responsible") so I said, with a slight sneer, "Please, just drop us at the hospital."

ALICE. Show me the sneer. *(Dan considers, then sneers.)* Very good. *Buster.*

DAN. We put you in the cab and came here.

ALICE. What was I doing?

DAN. You were murmuring, "I'm very sorry for all the inconvenience." I had my arm round you ... your head was on my shoulder.

ALICE. Was my head ... *lolling?*

DAN. That's exactly what it was doing.

(Pause.)

ALICE. You'll be late for work.

DAN. Are you saying you want me to go?

ALICE. I'm saying you'll be late for work.

(Beat.)

DAN. Why were you at Blackfriars Bridge?

ALICE. I'd been to a club near the meat market ... *Smithfield.* Do you go clubbing?

DAN. No, I'm too old.

ALICE. How old are you?
DAN. Thirty-five.
ALICE. Half-time?
DAN. Thank you very much. So, you were *clubbing* ...
ALICE. Then I went for a walk, I went to see the meat being unloaded.
DAN. The carcasses, why?
ALICE. Because they're repulsive.
Then I found this tiny park ... it's a graveyard too. *Postman's Park.*
Do you know it?
DAN. No.
ALICE. There's a memorial to ordinary people who died saving the lives of others.
It's most *curious.*
Then I decided to go to Borough — so I went to Blackfriars Bridge to cross the river.
DAN. That *park* ... it's near here?
ALICE. Yes.
DAN. Is there a ... statue?
ALICE. A Minotaur.
DAN. I do know it. We sat there ... (my mother's dead) ... my father and I sat there the afternoon she died.
She died *here*, actually. She was a smoker.
(Remembering.) My father ... ate ... an egg sandwich ... his hands shook with grief ... pieces of egg fell on the grass ... butter on his top lip.
But I don't remember a memorial.
ALICE. Is your father still alive?
DAN. Clinging on. He's in a home.
ALICE. How did you end up writing obituaries? What did you *really* want to be?
DAN. *(Smiles.)* Oh ... I had dreams of being a writer but I had no voice.
What am I saying? I had no *talent.*
So ... I ended up in the "Siberia" of journalism.
ALICE. Tell me what you do, I want to imagine you in Siberia.
DAN. Really?

ALICE. Yes.

(Beat.)

DAN. Well ... we call it "the obits page." There's three of us; me, Harry and *Graham.* When I get to work, without fail, Graham will say, "Who's on the slab?" Meaning, did anyone important die overnight — are you *sure* you want to know?

ALICE. Yes.

DAN. Well, if someone "important" did die we go to the "deep freeze" which is a computer containing all the obituaries and we'll find the dead person's life.

ALICE. People's obituaries are written when they're still alive?

DAN. Some people's.

If no one important has died then *Harry* — he's the editor — he decides who we lead with and we check facts, make calls, polish the prose.

Some days I might be asked to deal with the widows or widowers; they try to persuade us to run an obituary of their husbands or wives. They feel we're dishonouring their loved ones if we don't but ... most of them are ... well, there isn't the space.

At six, we stand round the computer and read the next day's page, make final changes, put in a few euphemisms to amuse ourselves ...

ALICE. Such as?

DAN. "He was a convivial fellow," meaning he was an alcoholic.

"He valued his privacy" — gay.

"He *enjoyed* his privacy" ... raging queen.

(Pause. Alice slowly strokes Dan's face. He is unnerved but not unwilling.)

ALICE. And what would *your* euphemism be?

DAN. *(Softly.)* For me?

ALICE. Mmm.

DAN. He was ... *reserved.*

ALICE. And mine?

DAN. She was ... *disarming.*

(Beat.)

ALICE. How did you get this job?

DAN. They ask you to write your own obituary: if it amuses, you're in. *(They are close. Looking at each other. Larry walks past in a white coat. Dan stops him.)*

DAN. Excuse me, we've been waiting quite a long time ...
LARRY. I'm sorry, it's not my ... *(Larry is about to walk away. He glances briefly at Alice. "Pretty girl." He stops.)*

What happened?

ALICE. I was hit by a cab.
DAN. She was unconscious for about ten seconds.
LARRY. May I? *(Larry looks at the wound and examines her leg with interest.)* You can feel your toes?
ALICE. Yes.
LARRY. What's this? *(Larry traces the line of a scar on her leg.)*
ALICE. It's a scar.
LARRY. Yes, I know it's a *scar*. How did you get it?
ALICE. In America. A truck. *(Larry looks at the scar.)*
LARRY. Awful job.
ALICE. I was in the middle of nowhere.
LARRY. You'll be fine. *(Larry makes to leave.)*
ALICE. Can I have one? *(Larry looks at her, she nods at his pocket.)* A cigarette. *(Larry takes out his pack of cigarettes and removes one. Alice reaches for it, he withdraws it.)*
LARRY. Don't smoke it here. *(He hands her the cigarette.)*
DAN. Thank you. *(Larry exits. Alice lights the cigarette.)*
ALICE. Want a drag?
DAN. Yes but no. What were you doing, in "the middle of nowhere"?
ALICE. Travelling.
(Beat.)
DAN. Alone?
ALICE. With ... a *male*.
(Beat.)
DAN. What happened to this male?
ALICE. I don't know, I ran away.
DAN. Where?
ALICE. New York.
DAN. Just like that?
ALICE. It's the only way to leave; "I don't love you anymore, good-bye."
DAN. Supposing you do still love them?
ALICE. You don't leave.

DAN. You've never left someone you still love?
ALICE. No.
(Beat.)
DAN. When did you come back?
ALICE. Yesterday.
DAN. Where are your belongings? *(Alice points to her rucksack.)*
ALICE. I'm a waif.
(Beat.)
DAN. Did you like New York?
ALICE. Sure.
DAN. Were you ... studying?
ALICE. *Stripping. (Alice looks at him.)* Look at your little eyes.
DAN. I can't see my little eyes.
ALICE. They're popping out. You're a cartoon.
(Beat.)
DAN. Were you ... "good" at it?
ALICE. *Exceptional.*
DAN. Why?
ALICE. I know what men want.
DAN. Really?
ALICE. Oh yes.
DAN. Tell me ... *(Alice considers.)*
ALICE. Men want a girl who looks like a boy.
They want to protect her but she must be a survivor.
And she must come ... like a *train* ... but with ... *elegance*.
What do *you* want?
(Pause.)
DAN. Who was this ... *male?*
ALICE. A customer. But once I was his he hated me stripping.
(Dan smiles.)
DAN. What do *you* want?
ALICE. To be loved.
DAN. That simple?
ALICE. It's a big want. *(Alice looks at him.)* Do you have a girlfriend?
DAN. Yeah, *Ruth* ... she's called Ruth. She's a linguist. *(Dan looks at Alice.)* Will you meet me after work?

ALICE. No, take the day off. Don't go and see *"who's on the slab."* I'll call in for you and say you're sick.
DAN. I *can't.*
ALICE. Don't be such a pussy.
DAN. I might be anyone, I might be a psychotic.
ALICE. I've met psychotics, you're not. *Phone.* *(She holds out her hand, Dan gives her his mobile.)*
DAN. Memory One. *(Alice punches in the number and pulls out the aerial with her teeth.)*
ALICE. Who do I speak to?
DAN. Harry Masters.
ALICE. What's your name?
DAN. Mr. Daniel Woolf. What's *your* name?
(Beat.)
ALICE. Alice. My name is Alice Ayres.

BLACKOUT

Scene 2

Anna's studio.

Late afternoon. June. (The following year.)

Anna stands behind her camera. Dan sits. Anna takes a shot.

ANNA. Good. *(Shot.)*
Don't move. *(Shots.)*
DAN. What was this building?
ANNA. A refuge for fallen women. *(Shot.)*
DAN. Wasn't there a river here?
ANNA. *The Fleet.* They built over it in the eighteenth century.
DAN. A buried river. *(Shot.)*

ANNA. If you stand on Blackfriars Bridge you can see where it comes out.
DAN. I think I will.
ANNA. You must. *(Shot.)*
Stay there. *(Shots.)*
It inspired an "urban legend" — a bit like the alligators in New York. People thought that pigs were breeding underground and then one day this big, fat boar swam out into the Thames and trotted off along the Embankment.
DAN. So it was true?
ANNA. No, it escaped. From *Smithfield.*
DAN. Pigs *swim?*
ANNA. Surprisingly well. *(Shots.)*
Relax. *(Anna changes film, adjusts a light, etc. Dan stands up.)*
DAN. Do you mind if I smoke?
ANNA. If you must.
DAN. I don't have to.
ANNA. Then don't. *(Anna looks at Dan.)* I liked your book.
DAN. Thanks ...
ANNA. When's it published?
DAN. Next year, how come you read it?
ANNA. Your publisher sent me a manuscript, I read it last night. You kept me up till *four.*
DAN. I'm flattered.
ANNA. Is your anonymous heroine based on someone real?
(Beat.)
DAN. She's ... someone called Alice.
ANNA. How does she feel about you stealing her life?
DAN. *Borrowing* her life. I'm dedicating the book to her, she's pleased. *(Dan is staring at her, Anna turns, looks at him.)*
(Pause.)
Do you exhibit?
ANNA. Next summer.
DAN. Portraits?
ANNA. Yes.
DAN. Of who?
(Beat.)
ANNA. Strangers. *(Anna gestures for him to sit again. She checks the light on him with a meter.)*

DAN. How do your strangers feel about *you* stealing *their* lives?
ANNA. *Borrowing. (Anna adjusts his hair.)*
DAN. Am I a stranger?
ANNA. No ... you're a job.
(Pause.)
DAN. You're beautiful.
(Beat.)
ANNA. No I'm not. *(Anna looks down the lens.)* Chin up, you're a sloucher. *(Shots.)*
DAN. You didn't find it obscene?
ANNA. What?
DAN. The book.
ANNA. No, I thought it was ... *accurate. (Shot.)*
DAN. About what?
ANNA. About sex. About love. *(Shot.)*
DAN. In what way?
ANNA. You *wrote* it.
DAN. But you *read* it. Till *four*. *(Dan looks at her, Anna looks down the lens.)*
ANNA. Don't raise your eyebrows, you look smug. *(Shot.)* Stand up. *(Dan stands up.)*
DAN. But you did *like* it?
ANNA. Yes, but I could go off it. *(Shots.)*
DAN. Any criticisms? *(Anna considers.)*
ANNA. Bad title.
DAN. Got a better one?
ANNA. Really?
DAN. Yeh ...
(Beat.)
ANNA. *The Aquarium. (They look at each other.)*
(Beat.).
DAN. You liked the dirty bit...?
ANNA. Some of it.
DAN. You like Aquariums?
ANNA. Fish are therapeutic.
DAN. Hang out in Aquariums, do you?
ANNA. When I can.
DAN. Good for picking up "Strangers"?

ANNA. *Photographing* strangers. I took my first picture in the one at London Zoo.
(Silence.)
DAN. *(Gently.)* Come here ...
(Pause. Anna moves towards him, slowly. She stops.)
ANNA. I don't kiss strange men.
DAN. Neither do I. *(They kiss. Ten seconds. Anna slowly pulls back.)*
ANNA. Do you and this ... *Alice* ... live together? *(Dan considers.)*
DAN. ... Yes ...
ANNA. *(Nods.)* "She has one address in her address book; ours ... under 'H' for home." *(Dan touches her face.)*
DAN. I've cut that line.
ANNA. Why?
DAN. Too sentimental. *(Anna gently takes his hand from her face, looks at it and then pulls away from him.)*
Are you married?
ANNA. Yes. *(Dan turns away, she looks at him.)*
No. *(Dan turns back.)*
Yes.
DAN. Which?
ANNA. Separated.
DAN. Do you have any children?
ANNA. No.
DAN. Would you like some?
ANNA. Yes, but not today. *(She shuts her camera case and begins to pack up, session over.)* Would *Alice* like children?
DAN. She's too young. *(Dan glances at his watch.)* Actually ... she's coming to meet me here ... quite soon.
ANNA. Why are you wasting her time?
DAN. I'm not. I'm grateful to her ... she's ... completely loveable and completely unleaveable.
ANNA. And you don't want someone else to get their dirty hands on her?
(Beat.)
DAN. Maybe.
ANNA. Men are crap.
DAN. But all the same ...

ANNA. They're still crap. *(The door buzzer goes.)* Your muse. *(Dan looks at Anna.)*
DAN. *(Ironic.)* You've ruined my life.
ANNA. You'll get over it. *(They look at each other. Dan goes to exit.)* Dan ... *(Dan turns.)* Your shirt. *(Dan exits, tucking his shirt into his trousers.)*
(Silence. Anna thinks. Dan enters with Alice. Her hair is a different colour from Scene 1.)
DAN. Anna ... Alice.
ANNA. Hi. *(Alice looks at Anna.)*
ALICE. I'm sorry if you're still working.
ANNA. No, we've just finished.
ALICE. Was he well-behaved?
ANNA. Reasonably.
ALICE. Is he photogenic?
ANNA. I think so.
ALICE. Did you steal his soul?
ANNA. Would you like some tea?
ALICE. No thanks, I've been serving it all day. Can I use the...?
ANNA. *(Gestures.)* Through there. *(Alice exits.)* *She* is beautiful.
DAN. Yes, she is. *(Dan looks at Anna.)* I've got to see you.
ANNA. No!
DAN. Why are you getting all ... "sisterly"?
ANNA. I'm not getting "sisterly," I don't want trouble.
DAN. I'm not trouble.
ANNA. You're taken.
(Pause.)
DAN. I've *got* to see you.
ANNA. *(Shakes her head.)* Tough.
(Pause. Alice enters.)
ALICE. I'm a block of ice. *(Dan goes to Alice and rubs her. To Anna.)* Will you take *my* photo?
I've never been photographed by a professional before.
I'd really appreciate it, I can pay you.
(Pause.)
ANNA. No ... I'd like to ...
ALICE. *(To Dan.)* Only if *you* don't mind.
DAN. Why should I?

ALICE. Because you'll have to go away. *(To Anna.)* We don't want *him* here while we're working, do we?
ANNA. No, we don't.
(Beat.)
DAN. ... *Right* ... I'll wait in the pub on the corner ... *(He kisses Alice.)* Have fun. *(To Anna.)* Thank you. Good luck with your exhibition.
ANNA. Good luck with your book.
DAN. Thanks. *(Dan exits, lighting a cigarette as he goes.)*
ALICE. You've got an exhibition?
ANNA. Only a small one. Take a seat. *(Alice sits. Anna busies herself with the camera, checks light, etc. Alice watches her.)*
I read Dan's book, you've had ... quite a life.
ALICE. Thanks.
Are you single?
ANNA. ... Yes.
ALICE. Who was your last boyfriend?
ANNA. *(Unsure where this is leading.)* My husband ...
ALICE. What happened to him?
(Beat.)
ANNA. Someone younger.
ALICE. What did he do?
ANNA. He made money. In the City.
ALICE. We used to get those in the clubs. *Wall Street boys.*
ANNA. So ... these places were quite ... upmarket?
ALICE. Some of them, but I preferred the dives.
ANNA. Why?
ALICE. The poor are more generous. *(Anna looks into the camera.)*
ANNA. You've got a great face. *(Anna focuses.)* How do you feel about Dan using your life, for his book?
ALICE. None of your fucking business. *(Alice stares at Anna.)* When he let me in ... downstairs, he had ... this ... "*look.*"
I just listened to your ... *conversation.*
(Silence.)
ANNA. I don't know what to say.
ALICE. *(Gently.)* Take my picture.
(Pause.)

ANNA. I'm not a thief, Alice. *(Anna looks down the lens.)*
Head up ... *(Alice raises her head, she is in tears.)*
You look beautiful. Turn to me ... *(Anna takes her shots. They look at each other.)*
Good.

BLACKOUT

Scene 3

Internet.

Early evening. January. (The following year.)

Dan is in his flat sitting at a table with a computer. There is a Newton's Cradle on the table. Writerly sloth, etc.

Larry is sitting at his hospital desk with a computer. He is wearing a white coat.

They are in separate rooms.

The scene is silent. Their "dialogue" appears on a large screen simultaneous to their typing it.

DAN. Hallo
LARRY. hi
DAN. How RU?
LARRY. ok
DAN. Cum here often?
LARRY. ?
DAN. Net
LARRY. 1st time
DAN. A Virgin. Welcome. What's your name?

LARRY. Larry. U? *(Dan considers.)*
DAN. Anna
LARRY. Nice 2 meet U
DAN. I love COCK
(Pause.)
LARRY. Youre v.forward
DAN. And UR chatting on "LONDON FUCK." Do U want sex?
LARRY. yes. describe u.
DAN. Dark hair. Dirty mouth. Epic Tits.
LARRY. define epic
DAN. 36DD
LARRY. Nice arse?
DAN. Y
LARRY. Becos i want 2 know *(Dan smiles.)*
DAN. No, "Y" means "Yes."
LARRY. O
DAN. I want 2 suck U senseless.
LARRY. B my guest
DAN. Sit on my face Fuckboy.
LARRY. I'm there
DAN. Wear my wet knickers.
(Beat.)
LARRY. ok
DAN. RU well hung?
LARRY. 9£

(Speaking.) Shit.

(Typing.) 9"

DAN. GET IT OUT. *(Larry considers and then unzips. He puts his hand in his trousers. The phone on his desk rings. Loud. He jumps.)*
LARRY. *(Speaking.)* Wait.

(Typing.) wait *(Larry picks up the phone. Dan lights a cigarette.)*

(Speaking.) Yes. What's the histology? *Progressive?* Sounds like an atrophy. *(Larry puts the phone down and goes back to his keyboard. Dan clicks the balls on his Newton's Cradle.)*

hallo? *(Dan looks at his screen.)*

anna

(Speaking.) Bollocks.

(Typing.) ANNA? WHERE RU?

DAN. Hey, big Larry, what d'you wank about? *(Larry considers.)*
LARRY. Ex-girlfriends
DAN. Not current g-friends?
LARRY. Never *(Dan smiles.)*
DAN. Tell me your sex-ex fantasy ...
LARRY. Hotel room ... they tie me up ... tease me ... won't let me come. They fight over me, 6 tonges on my cock, ballls, perineum etc.
DAN. All hail the Sultan of Twat? *(Larry laughs.)*
LARRY. Anna, wot do U wank about? *(Dan thinks.)*
DAN. Strangers.
LARRY. details ...
DAN. They form a Q and I attend to them like a cum hungry bitch, 1 in each hole and both hands.
LARRY. then?
DAN. They cum in my mouth arse tits cunt hair.
LARRY. *(Speaking.)* Jesus. *(Larry's phone rings. He picks up the receiver and replaces it without answering. Then he takes it off the hook.)* *(Typing.)* then?
DAN. i lik it off like the dirty slut I am. Wait,have to type with 1 hand ... I'm cumming right now ...

ohohohohohohohohohohohohohohohoho

ooooooooooooooooooooooooooooooooooooooooooooooooo

+_)(*&^%$£"!_*)&%^&!"!"£$%%^^%&^%&&*&*((*(*)&^%^*((£££

(Pause. Larry, motionless, stares at his screen.)
LARRY. was it good?
DAN. No. *(Larry shakes his head.)*
LARRY. I'm shocked
DAN. PARADISE SHOULD BE SHOCKING
LARRY. RU4 real?
(Beat.)
DAN. MEET ME
(Pause.)
LARRY. serious?
DAN. Y
LARRY. when

DAN. NOW

LARRY. can't. I'm a Dr. Must do rounds. *(Dan smiles. Larry flicks through his desk diary.)*

DAN. Dont b a pussy. Life without riskisdeath. Desire, like the world, is am accident. The bestsex is anon. We liv as we dream, ALONE. I'll make u cum like a train.

LARRY. Tomorrow, 1pm, where? *(Dan thinks.)*

DAN. The Aquarium, London Zoo & then HOTEL.

LARRY. How will U know me?

DAN. Bring white coat

LARRY. ?

DAN. Dr + Coat = Horn 4 me

LARRY. !

DAN. I send U a rose my love ...

LARRY. ?

DAN.
```
(@)
 |
\|
 |/
 |
 |
```

LARRY. Thanks. CU at Aquarium. Bye Anna.

DAN. Bye Larry xxxxx

LARRY. xxxxxx (*They look at their screens.)*

BLACKOUT

Scene 4

Aquarium.

Afternoon. January. (The next day.)

Anna is sitting on a bench, alone. She has a camera. She looks at the fish, occasionally referring to her guidebook.

Larry enters. He sees Anna. He checks her out and smiles. Anna sees him and vaguely nods, acknowledging his presence.

LARRY. Anna?
ANNA. ... Yes...? *(Larry unbuttons his overcoat and holds it open. He is wearing his white coat underneath.)*
LARRY. I've got "The Coat." (*Anna observes him.)*
ANNA. Yes, you *have.*
LARRY. "The White Coat."
ANNA. So I see ...
LARRY. I'm Larry. *(Dirty.)* "The Doctor."
(Beat.)
ANNA. Hallo, Doctor Larry.
LARRY. Feel free to call me ... *"The Sultan."*
ANNA. *Why?*
LARRY. *(Laughs.)* I can't believe these things actually happen.
I thought ... if you turned up, you'd be a bit of a trout ... but you're bloody *gorgeous.*
ANNA. Thanks.
(Beat.)
LARRY. You mentioned a hotel ... *(Anna looks at him, trying to work out who he is.)*
No rush. *(Larry checks his watch.)*
Actually, there *is,* I've got to be in surgery by three.
ANNA. Are you having an operation?

LARRY. *(Laughs.)* No, I'm *doing* one.

ANNA. You really are a doctor?

LARRY. I said I was. *(Sudden panic.)* You are ... *Anna?*

ANNA. Yes. I'm sorry, have we met somewhere?

LARRY. Don't play games, you ... "Nymph of the Net." *(Confused.)* You were filthy *yesterday.*

ANNA. Was I?

LARRY. YES. "Wear my wet knickers," "Sit on my face," "I'm a cum-hungry bitch typing with one ... " *(Anna smiles.)* Why do I feel like a pervert?

ANNA. I think ... you're the victim ... of a medic's prank. *(Pause.)*

LARRY. I am *so* sorry. *(Larry exits. Anna chuckles. Larry reenters.)* NO. We spoke on the Net but now you've *seen* me you don't ... it's *fine,* I'm not going to get upset about it.

ANNA. Then why are you upset?

LARRY. I'm not, I'm frustrated.

ANNA. I don't even have a computer, I'm a photographer. *(Larry considers.)*

LARRY. Where were *you* between the hours of 5.45 and 6.00 P.M., yesterday?

ANNA. I was in a cafe seeing ... an acquaintance.

LARRY. Name?

ANNA. Alice Ayres.

LARRY. The nature of your business?

ANNA. *(Amused.)* Photographic business. Where were *you* between those hours?

LARRY. On the Net talking to you.

ANNA. No.

LARRY. Well I was talking to *someone.*

ANNA. *(Realizing.)* Pretending to *be* me. You were talking to Daniel Woolf.

LARRY. Who?

ANNA. He's Alice's boyfriend. She told me yesterday that he plays around on the Net. It's *him.*

LARRY. No, I was talking to a woman.

ANNA. How do you know?
LARRY. Because ... believe me, she was a woman, I got a *huge* ... She was a woman.
ANNA. No, she wasn't.
LARRY. She wasn't, was she.
ANNA. No.
LARRY. What a CUNT. Sorry.
ANNA. I'm a grown-up, "Cunt Away."
LARRY. Thanks. This ... "*bloke*" ...
ANNA. Daniel Woolf.
LARRY. How do you know him?
ANNA. I don't know him really, I took his photo for a book he wrote.
LARRY. I hope it sank without a trace.
ANNA. It's on its way.
LARRY. There is justice in the world. What's it called?
ANNA. *(Smiles.) The Aquarium.*
LARRY. What a PRICK. He's advertising.
Why? Why would he pretend to be you?
ANNA. He likes me.
LARRY. Funny way of showing it, can't he send you flowers? *(Larry produces a crumpled rose from his coat pocket. He hands it to Anna.)* Here.
ANNA. ... Thanks ... *(Anna looks at the rose, then at Larry.)*
Wonderful thing, the Internet.
LARRY. Oh yes.
ANNA. The possibility of genuine global communication, the last great democratic medium.
LARRY. Absolutely, it's the future.
ANNA. Two boys tossing in cyberspace.
LARRY. *He* was the tosser.
I'll say this for him, he can *write. (Larry looks at Anna.)* Is he in love with you?
ANNA. I don't know. No.
LARRY. Are you in love with him?
ANNA. I hardly know him, no.
LARRY. But you're sort of ... interested?
ANNA. I think he's ... *interesting.*

(Beat.)
LARRY. So what are you doing here?
(Pause.)
ANNA. Looking at fish. *(Anna looks away from him.)*
LARRY. *(Gently.)* Are you all right? *(Anna nods.)* You can tell me ...
ANNA. Because you're a doctor?
LARRY. Because I'm *here.* *(Anna turns to him.)* Crying is allowed.
ANNA. I'm not allowed. Thanks, anyway.
LARRY. I'm famed for my bedside manner. *(Anna raises her camera, Larry covers his face.)* Don't, I look like a criminal in photos.
ANNA. Please, it's my birthday.
LARRY. *(Dropping his hands.)* Really? *(Anna takes his photo.)*
ANNA. Yes. *(Rueful.)* *Really.* *(They look at each other.)*
LARRY. Happy Birthday.

BLACKOUT

Scene 5

Gallery.

Evening. June. (Five months later.)

Alice is looking at a huge photograph of herself. She has a bottle of lager. She wears a black dress.

Dan has a glass of wine. A slightly shabby black suit. He looks at Alice looking at the image.

DAN. Cheers. *(She turns. They drink. Dan admires the photo.)* You're the belle of the bullshit. You look beautiful.
ALICE. I'm *here.* *(Dan looks at Alice, smiles.)* A man came into the cafe today and said, "Hey, *waitress,* what are you waiting for?"

DAN. Funny guy.
ALICE. I said, "I'm waiting for a man to come in here and *fuck me sideways* with a beautiful line like that."
DAN. *(Smiles.)* What did he do?
ALICE. He asked for a cup of tea with two sugars. *(Alice looks at him.)* I'm waiting for *you.*
DAN. To do what?
(Beat.)
ALICE. *(Gently.)* Leave me.
DAN. *(Concerned.)* I'm not going to leave you. I totally love you. What is this?
ALICE. Please let me come ... *(Dan turns away.)* I want to *be there* for you. Are you ashamed of me?
DAN. Of course not. I've told you, I want to be alone.
ALICE. Why?
DAN. To *grieve* ... to think.
ALICE. I love you, why won't you let me?
DAN. It's only a weekend.
ALICE. Why won't you let me *love* you?
(Silence.)
We've never spent a weekend in the country.
DAN. Well ... we will. *(Dan turns, drinks. He looks offstage and smiles at something he sees.)*
Harry's here ... pissed as a newt.
He wants me to go back to "obits" ... says they miss me.
ALICE. Poor Harry, you know he's in love with you.
DAN. No he's not. *(Dan glances offstage again.)* Is he?
ALICE. *(Smiles.)* Yes. Do you want to go back?
DAN. We're very poor ...
ALICE. What about your writing? *(Dan shrugs.)*
DAN. Look ... I'm going to say hallo and good-bye to Anna and then I'll get a cab to the station, OK?
Buster?
I love you. *(Dan kisses her forehead.)*
ALICE. *(Softly.)* Kiss my lips ...
DAN. Sorry. *(Dan kisses her on the lips.)* I'll call you as soon as I get there. *(Dan exits as Larry enters. They almost collide. Larry regards the departing Dan. Alice lights a cigarette, she uses her bottle as an ash-*

tray. Larry is wearing a suit with a black cashmere sweater with a collar. He has a bottle of wine and a glass. Alice looks at him, curious.)

LARRY. Evening.

ALICE. Are you a waiter?

LARRY. No, I'm a refugee escaping from the glittering babble. *(Larry looks at the photo and then at his exhibition price list.)*

And ... *you* are ... "*Young Woman, London.*" *(Larry looks at Alice.)* *Pricey*. Do you like it?

ALICE. No.

LARRY. Well you should. What were you so sad about?

ALICE. Life.

LARRY. What's that then? *(Alice smiles. Larry gestures to the photos.)* What d'you reckon, in general?

ALICE. You want to talk about *art?*

LARRY. I know it's *vulgar* to discuss "The Work" at an opening of "The Work" but *someone's* got to do it. Serious, what d'you think?

ALICE. It's a lie.

It's a bunch of sad strangers photographed beautifully and all the rich fuckers who appreciate *art* say it's beautiful because that's what they want to see.

But the people in the photos are sad and alone but the pictures make the world *seem* beautiful.

So, the exhibition is reassuring, which makes it a lie, and everyone loves a Big Fat Lie.

LARRY. I'm the Big Fat Liar's boyfriend.

ALICE. Bastard.

LARRY. Larry.

ALICE. Alice.

(Beat. Alice moves in on him.)

So ... you're Anna's boyfriend?

LARRY. A princess can kiss a frog.

ALICE. How long have you been seeing her?

LARRY. Four months. We're in "the first flush."

It's Paradise. All my nasty habits amuse her ... *(He gazes at Alice.)* You shouldn't smoke.

ALICE. Fuck off.

LARRY. I'm a doctor, I'm supposed to say things like that. *(Alice now realizes where she's seen him before. She holds out her packet of cigarettes.)*

ALICE. Want one?

LARRY. No. *(Alice continues to offer the packet.)*

Yes. No. Fuck it, yes. NO. I've given up. *(Larry watches her smoking.)*

Pleasure and self-destruction, the perfect poison. *(Alice gives him a dirty smile.)*

Anna told me your bloke wrote a book, any good?

ALICE. Of course.

LARRY. It's about *you,* isn't it?

ALICE. Some of me.

LARRY. Oh? What did he leave out?

(Beat.)

ALICE. The truth.

(Beat.)

LARRY. Is he here? Your *bloke.*

ALICE. Yeah, he's talking to your *bird.* *(Larry glances offstage, thinks, then returns to Alice.)*

LARRY. *So* ... you were a stripper?

ALICE. *(Flirtatious.)* Yeah ... and? *(Larry sees the scar on her leg.)*

LARRY. Mind if I ask how you got that?

(Beat.)

ALICE. You've asked me this before.

LARRY. When?

ALICE. Two and a half years ago. I was in hospital. You looked at my leg.

LARRY. How did you remember me?

ALICE. It was a memorable day.

You didn't really want to stop but you did, you were off for a crafty smoke.

You gave me a cigarette.

LARRY. Well, I don't smoke now and nor should you.

ALICE. But you *used* to go and smoke. *On the sly.*

LARRY. Yeah, in a little park near the hospital.
ALICE. *Postman's Park?*
LARRY. That's the one. *(Alice takes a swig from his bottle.)* And ... the *scar?*
ALICE. A Mafia hit man broke my leg.
LARRY. *(Disbelieving.)* Really?
ALICE. Absolutely.
LARRY. Doesn't look like a break ...
ALICE. What does it look like?
LARRY. Like something went into it. *(Tentative.)* A knife, maybe ...
ALICE. When I was eight ... some metal went into my leg when my parents' car crashed ... when they *died.* Happy now?
LARRY. Sorry, it was none of my business. I'm supposed to be off-duty. *(Alice looks at him.)*
ALICE. Is it nice being good?
LARRY. I'm not good. *(Larry looks at her, close.)* What about *you? (Larry gently strokes her face, she lets him.)* I'm seeing my first private patient tomorrow. Tell me I'm not a sellout.
ALICE. You're not a sellout.
LARRY. *Thanks.* You take care.
ALICE. I will, you too. *(Alice exits. Larry watches her go. Larry exits as Dan enters elsewhere. Dan carries a small suitcase. He checks his watch and waits, nervously. Anna enters. Pause. They look at each other.)*
ANNA. I can't talk for long.
DAN. Bit of a do, isn't it?
ANNA. Yeah, I hate it.
DAN. But you're *good* at it.

So, he's a *dermatologist.* Can you get more boring than that?
ANNA. Obituarist?
DAN. Failed novelist, please.
ANNA. I was sorry about your book.
DAN. Thanks, I blame the title.
ANNA. *(Smiles.)* I blame the critics. You must write another one.
DAN. Why can't failure be attractive?
ANNA. It's not a failure.
DAN. It's *perceived* to be, therefore it is. Pathetically, I needed praise. A *real* writer is ... above such concerns.
ANNA. Romantic tosh.

DAN. Ever had bad reviews? Well, shut up then.
Talk to *Doctor Larry* about photography, do you?
Is he a fan of Man Ray or Karsh?
He'll *bore* you.
ANNA. No he won't — he doesn't, actually.
DAN. *(Exasperated.)* I cannot believe I made this happen.
What were you doing at the Aquarium?
(Joking.) Thinking of me?
ANNA. No. How's Alice?
DAN. She's fine. Do you love him?
ANNA. Yes, very much.
(Beat.)
DAN. *(Alarmed.)* You're not going to *marry* him?
ANNA. I might.
DAN. *Don't.* Marry me. Children, everything.
You don't want his children — three little stooges in white coats.
Don't marry him, marry me.
Grow old with me ... *die* with me ... wear a battered cardigan on the beach in Bournemouth.
Marry me.
ANNA. *(Smiles.)* I don't *know* you.
DAN. Yes you do.
I couldn't feel what I feel for you unless you felt it too.
Anna, *we're in love* — it's not our fault, stop wasting his time.
ANNA. I haven't *seen* you for a year.
DAN. Yes you have.
ANNA. Only because you *stalked* me outside my studio.
DAN. I didn't stalk ... I ... *lurked.*
And when I wasn't there you looked for me.
ANNA. How do you know, if you weren't *there?*
DAN. Because I was there ... lurking from a distance.
(I love your work by the way, it's tragic.)
ANNA. *(Sarcastic.)* Thanks. *(Dan gestures to his suitcase.)*
DAN. I know this isn't "appropriate," I'm going to my father's funeral — come with me.

ANNA. Your father died?
DAN. It's fine, I hated him — no, I didn't — I don't care, I *care* about THIS.

Come with me, spend a weekend with me, then decide.

ANNA. I don't want to go to your father's funeral.

There's nothing *to* ... *decide.*

What about Alice?

DAN. She'll survive.

I can't be her father anymore.

Anna, you want to believe he's ... "the one" ... it's not *real,* you're scared of *this.*

ANNA. There is no "this." I Love him.

DAN. *Why?*

ANNA. Any number of reasons.

DAN. Name *one.*

ANNA. He's kind.

DAN. *(Ferocious.)* Don't give me "kind." "Kind" is *dull,* "kind" will kill you. Alice is "*kind,*" even *I'm* "kind," anyone can be fucking KIND.

(Gently.) I cannot live without you.

ANNA. You can ... you *do.*

(Beat.)

DAN. This is not me, I don't do this.

All the language is old, there are no new words ... *I love you.*

(Beat.)

ANNA. No, you don't.

DAN. Yes ... I do. I *need* you.

I can't think, I can't work, I can't *breathe.*

We are going to *die.*

Please ... *save* me.

Look at me. *(Anna looks at Dan.)*

Tell me you're not in love with me.

(Beat.)

ANNA. I'm not in love with you.

(Pause.)

DAN. You just lied.

See me next week. *Please,* Anna ... I'm begging you ...

I'm your stranger ... *jump.*

(Silence. They are very close. Larry has entered, he is looking at them. Dan sees him and goes to exit.)

ANNA. Your case. *(Dan returns, picks up his suitcase and exits.)*

(Pause.)

LARRY. Hallo ... *Stranger.*

ANNA. Hallo.

LARRY. Intense conversation?

(Beat.)

ANNA. His father's died. Were you *spying?*

LARRY. Lovingly *observing* — (with a telescope). *(Larry kisses Anna.)* He's taller than his photo.

ANNA. The photo's a head shot.

LARRY. Yeah, I know, but his head *implied* a short body ... but in fact, his head is ... deceptive.

ANNA. Deceptive?

LARRY. Yes, because he's actually got a *long* body. He's a stringy fucker. *(Anna laughs.)* I could 'ave 'im.

ANNA. *What?*

LARRY. If it came to it, in a scrap, I could 'ave 'im. *(Anna smiles.)* Did you tell him we call him "Cupid"?

ANNA. No, that's *our* joke. *(Anna tugs his sweater, pulling him towards her.)*

LARRY. I've never worn cashmere before. Thank you. I'm Cinderella at the ball.

ANNA. *(Charmed.)* You're such a peasant.

LARRY. You love it. *(Larry holds her.)*

I had a chat with young Alice.

ANNA. Fancy her?

LARRY. 'Course. Not as much as *you.*

ANNA. Why?

LARRY. You're a woman ... she's a girl.

She has the moronic beauty of youth but she's got ... *side.*

ANNA. She seems very open to me.

LARRY. That's how she *wants* to seem. You forget you're dealing with a clinical observer of the human carnival.

ANNA. Am I now?

LARRY. Oh yes.

ANNA. You seem more like "the cat who got the cream." You can stop licking yourself, you know.
(Pause. Anna turns to Larry, slowly.)
LARRY. *(Coolly.)* That's the nastiest thing you've ever said to me.
ANNA. God, I'm sorry. It was a horrible thing to say. It's just ... my family's here and friends ...
I have no excuse. I'm sorry.
(Pause.)
LARRY. Forget it. I know what you mean. I'll stop pawing you. *(Anna kisses him.)* I met your *dad* ...
ANNA. I know. He actually said, "I like him." He's never said that before ... about *anyone.* They all adored you; my stepmother thinks you're gorgeous,
"Lovely hands," she said, "you can imagine him doing his stitching, very sensitively."
LARRY. So they didn't think I was "beneath you"?
ANNA. *No.* You're not ... you're *you* and you're wonderful. *(Larry holds her.)*
LARRY. Did you like my folks? They loved *you.*
ANNA. Your mother's got such a ... kind face. *(They look at each other.)*

BLACKOUT

Scene 6

Domestic interiors.

Midnight. June. (A year later.)

Anna sitting on a chaise longue.

Alice asleep, curled up on a small sofa. She is wearing striped pyjamas. A half-eaten red apple beside her.

They are in separate rooms.

Dan enters. He carries the brown briefcase seen in Scene 1. He looks at Alice. After a while she wakes.

ALICE. Where've you been?
What?
DAN. Work. I had a drink with Harry. You never have *one* drink with Harry.
ALICE. Did you eat? I made sandwiches — no crusts.
DAN. I'm not hungry.
(Pause.)
ALICE. *What?*
(Beat.)
DAN. This will hurt.
I've been with Anna.
I'm in love with her. We've been seeing each other for a year.
(Silence. Alice gets up and slowly exits. On the other side of the stage Larry enters. He has a suitcase, bags, duty-free carrier.)
LARRY. *(To Anna.)* Don't move.
I want to remember this moment forever; the first time I walked through the door, returning from a business trip, to be greeted by my *wife*.
I have, in this moment, become an adult. *(Larry kisses Anna.)*
Thanks for waiting up, you darling. You goddess.

I missed you.

Jesus, I'm knackered.

ANNA. Didn't you sleep on the plane?

LARRY. No, because the permed German sleeping next to me was snoring like a *Messerschmitt. (Larry removes his jacket, Anna takes it.)* What's the time?

ANNA. Midnight.

LARRY. Seven.

Time — what a tricky little fucker.

My head's in two places, my brain actually *hurts.*

ANNA. Do you want some food?

LARRY. Nahh, I ate my "Scooby Snacks" on the plane. I need a bath.

ANNA. Shall I run you one?

LARRY. No, I'll just have a shower. *(Larry untucks his shirt and kicks off his shoes.)* You OK?

ANNA. Mmhmm.

(Beat. They look at each other.)

How was the ... *thing?*

LARRY. As Dermatological Conferences go, it was a riot. *(Larry takes a bottle of Scotch from his bag of duty-free and swigs it.)*

ANNA. How was the hotel?

LARRY. Someone told me that the beautiful people of "*The Paramount Hotel,*" the concierge and the bell boys and girls — did you know this? They're all *whores.*

ANNA. Everyone knows that.

LARRY. *I* didn't. Want some? *(Larry offers the bottle, Anna takes a swig.)*

I *love* New York. What a town: it's a twenty-four-hour pageant called, "Whatever You Want." They *celebrate* the sellout, it's a Mardi Gras of degradation.

Then, you arrive back at Heathrow and the first thing you see is this ... *carpet.*

This Unbelievable Carpet.

What the fuck colour is the carpet at Heathrow Airport?

They must've layed it to reassure foreigners we're not a serious country.

God I stink.

ANNA. Are you all right?
LARRY. Yeah. I don't suppose you fancy a friendly poke?
(Beat.)
ANNA. I've just had a bath.
LARRY. I'll see to myself then, in the *Elle Decoration* bathroom.
ANNA. You chose that bathroom.
LARRY. Yeah and every time I wash in it I feel *dirty.* It's *cleaner* than I am. It's got attitude. The mirror says, "Who the fuck are you?"
ANNA. You chose it.
LARRY. Doesn't mean I like it. We shouldn't have ... *this. (Larry gestures vaguely about the room.)*
ANNA. Are you experiencing bourgeois guilt?
(Beat.)
LARRY. *(Sharp.)* Working-class guilt. *(Larry looks at Anna.)* Why are you dressed? If you've just had a bath.
(Beat.)
ANNA. We needed some milk.
LARRY. Right. *(Larry goes to exit, stops.)* You OK?
ANNA. Uh-huh. You?
LARRY. Yeah ... *(Larry exits. Alice enters. She is wearing the black coat from Scene 1, also her rucksack from the same scene.)*
ALICE. I'm going.
DAN. I'm sorry.
ALICE. Irrelevant. What are you sorry for?
(Beat.)
DAN. Everything.
ALICE. Why didn't you tell me before?
(Beat.)
DAN. Cowardice.
ALICE. Is it because she's clever?
DAN. No, it's because ... she doesn't need me.
(Pause.)
ALICE. Do you bring her here?
DAN. Yes.
ALICE. She sits here?

DAN. Yes.

(Beat.)

ALICE. Didn't she get *married?*

DAN. She stopped seeing me.

(Beat.)

ALICE. Is that when we went to the country? To celebrate our third anniversary?

DAN. Yes.

ALICE. At least have the guts to look at me. *(Dan looks at her.)*
Did you phone her? To beg her to come back? When you went for your "long, *lonely* walks"?

DAN. Yes.

ALICE. You're a piece of shit.

DAN. Deception is brutal, I'm not pretending otherwise.

ALICE. How...? How does it *work?* How can you do this to someone?

(Silence.)

DAN. I don't know.

ALICE. Not good enough, I'm going. *(Dan prevents her from leaving.)*

DAN. It's late, it's not *safe* out there.

ALICE. And it's *safe* in here?

DAN. What about your things?

ALICE. I don't need "things."

DAN. Where will you go?

ALICE. I'll disappear. *(Larry enters having had his shower. He is wearing a dressing gown. He hands Anna a shoe box.)*

LARRY. "The Sultan" has returned bearing gifts. *(Anna opens the box and takes out the shoes. Dan moves towards Alice.)*

ALICE. DON'T COME NEAR ME.

ANNA. *(To Larry.)* They're beautiful. Thank you. *(Larry kisses Anna.)*

LARRY. Hey, guess what, *Alice* was at the Paramount Hotel.

ANNA. What?

LARRY. They sell arty postcards in the lobby, I bought one to boost your sales. *(Larry takes a postcard from his dressing gown pocket and reads the back.)*
"Young Woman, London." *(Larry hands the postcard to Anna.)*

And ... I checked for your book in The Museum of Modern Art. It's *there*. Someone bloody bought one! This *student* with a ridiculous little beard, he was drooling over your photo on the inside cover — fancied you, the *Geek*. I was so proud of you — "You've Broken New York."

ANNA. You're wonderful.

LARRY. Don't ever forget it. *(Larry exits.)*

ALICE. Change your mind.

Please, change your mind.

Can I still see you?

Dan ... can I still *see* you?

Answer me.

DAN. I can't see you. If I see you I'll never leave you.

(Beat.)

ALICE. What will you do if *I* find someone else?

DAN. Be jealous.

(Beat.)

ALICE. Do you still fancy me?

DAN. Of course. *(Alice shakes her head.)*

ALICE. You're lying. I've been "*you.*" *(Alice starts to cry.)*

Hold me? *(Dan holds her.)* I amuse you but I bore you.

DAN. No. *No.*

ALICE. You did love me?

DAN. I'll *always* love you. You changed my life. I hate hurting you.

ALICE. So why are you?

DAN. Because ... I'm selfish and I think I'll be happier with her.

ALICE. You won't, you'll miss me. No one will ever love you as much as I do.

DAN. I know.

(Pause.)

ALICE. Why isn't love enough?

I'm the one who leaves.

I'm supposed to leave *you.*

I'm the one who leaves. *(Alice kisses Dan. He responds. She breaks.)*

Make some tea ... *Buster. (Dan exits. Alice and Anna are alone.*

Larry enters. He is wearing trousers and the black cashmere seen in Scene 5.)

ANNA. Why are you dressed?

LARRY. Because I think you might be about to leave me and I didn't want to be wearing a dressing gown.

I slept with someone in New York.

A whore.

I'm sorry.

Please don't leave me.

(Beat.)

ANNA. Why?

LARRY. For sex. I wanted *sex.* (I wore a condom.)

(Beat.)

ANNA. Was it ... good? *(Larry huffs and puffs.)*

LARRY. ... Yes ...

ANNA. "*Paramount*" whore?

LARRY. No ... Forty ... something street.

ANNA. Where did you go?

LARRY. Her place.

ANNA. Nice?

LARRY. Not as nice as ours. I'm really sorry.

(Pause.)

ANNA. Why did you tell me?

LARRY. I couldn't lie to you.

ANNA. Why not?

LARRY. Because I love you.

(Pause.)

ANNA. It's fine.

LARRY. Really? *Why? (Anna looks at her shoes.)*

ANNA. Guilt present?

LARRY. Love present. Something's wrong ...

Anna ... *(Anna turns to him.)*

Are you leaving me? *(Anna nods.)*

Why?

ANNA. Dan.

(Beat.)

LARRY. "Cupid"? He's our *joke.*

ANNA. I love him.

(Pause.)

LARRY. You're seeing him now ...

ANNA. Yes.

LARRY. Since when?

ANNA. Since my opening, last year. I'm disgusting.

(Beat.)

LARRY. You're *phenomenal* ... you're so ... clever.

Why did you marry me?

ANNA. I stopped seeing him, I wanted us to work.

LARRY. *(Tough.)* Why did you tell me you wanted children?

ANNA. Because I did.

LARRY. And now you want children with him?

ANNA. Yes — I don't know — I'm so sorry.

(Pause.)

LARRY. *Why?*

(Beat.)

ANNA. I need him.

(Silence.)

LARRY. But ... we're happy ... aren't we?

ANNA. Yes.

(Beat.)

LARRY. Are you going to live with him?

ANNA. Yes. You stay here, if you want to.

LARRY. I don't give a FUCK about "the spoils." *(Alice exits with her rucksack.)* You did this the day we met; let me *hang* myself for your amusement.

Why didn't you tell me the second I walked in the door?

ANNA. I was scared.

LARRY. Because you're a coward. You spoilt *bitch*. *(Dan enters with two cups of tea, he sees Alice has gone. He exits after her.)*

Are you dressed because you thought I might hit you? *(Larry moves towards Anna, slowly. Close.)* What do you think I *am?*

ANNA. I've been hit before.

LARRY. Not by me. *(Larry stands over Anna.)* Is he a good fuck?

ANNA. Don't do this.

LARRY. Just answer the question. Is he *good?*

(Beat.)

ANNA. Yes.
LARRY. Better than me?
ANNA. Different.
LARRY. Better?
ANNA. Gentler.
LARRY. What does that mean?
ANNA. You know what it means.
LARRY. *Tell me.*
ANNA. No.
LARRY. I treat you like a whore?
ANNA. Sometimes.
LARRY. Why would that be?
(Silence.)
ANNA. I'm sorry, you're —
LARRY. Don't say it, don't fucking say, "You're too good for me." I *am* — but don't say it.
(Larry kneels to her. Gently.) Anna, you're making the mistake of your life.
You're leaving me because you think you don't deserve happiness, but you do Anna, you do ... *(Larry looks at her).*
Did you have a bath because you had sex with him? *(Anna looks at him. He moves away from her.)*
So you didn't smell of him? So you'd feel less *guilty?*
And how do you *feel?*
ANNA. Guilty.
(Beat.)
LARRY. Did you *ever* love me?
ANNA. *Yes.*
LARRY. Big fucking deal.
(Silence. Larry breaks down.)
Anna ... please, don't leave me ... *please. (Anna holds Larry. On the other side of the stage Dan reenters and sits on the sofa.)*
Did you do it here?
ANNA. No.
LARRY. Why not? *(Larry breaks from her. Hard.)* Just tell me the truth.
(Beat.)
ANNA. Yes, we did it here.

LARRY. Where?
(Beat.)
ANNA. Here.
LARRY. On this? *(He gestures to the chaise longue.)*
We had our first fuck on this.
Think of *me?*
When?
When did you do it here?
ANSWER THE FUCKING QUESTION.
(Beat.)
ANNA. *(Scared.)* This evening.
(Pause.)
LARRY. Did you come?
ANNA. Why are you doing this?
LARRY. Because I want to know.
(Beat.)
ANNA. *(Softly.)* Yes ... I came.
LARRY. How many times?
ANNA. Twice.
LARRY. How?
ANNA. First he went down on me and then we fucked.
(Beat.)
LARRY. Who was where?
ANNA. *(Tough.)* I was on top and then he fucked me from behind.
LARRY. And that's when you came the second time?
ANNA. *Why is the sex so important?*
LARRY. BECAUSE I'M A FUCKING CAVEMAN.
Did you touch yourself while he fucked you?
ANNA. Yes.
LARRY. You wank for him?
ANNA. Sometimes.
LARRY. And he does?
ANNA. We do everything that people who have sex do.
LARRY. You enjoy sucking him off?
ANNA. *Yes.*
LARRY. You like his cock?

ANNA. I love it.
LARRY. You like him coming in your face?
ANNA. *Yes*.
LARRY. What does it taste like?
ANNA. It tastes like you but *sweeter*.
LARRY. *THAT's* the *spirit.* Thank you. Thank you for your *honesty*.
Now fuck off and die. You fucked-up slag.

BLACKOUT

ACT TWO

Scene 7

Lapdance Club.

Late night. September. (Three months later.)

Larry is sitting. He is wearing a smart suit.

Alice is standing. She is wearing a short dress, wig and high heels. She has a garter round her thigh, there is cash in the garter.

They are in a private room. Music in the distance.

Larry gazes at her. She smiles. She is nice to him.

Silence.

LARRY. I love you.
(Pause.)
ALICE. Thank you.
(Beat.)
LARRY. What's this room called?
ALICE. "The Paradise Suite."
LARRY. How many Paradise Suites are there?
ALICE. Six.
(Beat.)
LARRY. Do I have to pay you to talk to me?

ALICE. No but if you want to tip me it's your choice. *(He takes out a twenty. She presents her leg. He puts the money in her garter.)* Thank you.

LARRY. I went to a place like this in New York. This is *swish.*
Pornography has gone upmarket — BULLY FOR ENGLAND.
This is honest *progress,* don't you think?

ALICE. England always imports the best of America.

LARRY. I used to come here twenty years ago ... it was a punk club ... the stage was ... *(Larry can't remember, he gives up.)*
Everything is a Version of Something Else. *(Larry takes a slug of his drink.)*
Twenty years ago, how old were *you?*

ALICE. Four.

LARRY. Christ, when I was in flares you were in nappies.

ALICE. My nappies were flared. *(Larry laughs.)*

LARRY. You have the face of an angel.

ALICE. Thank you.

LARRY. What does your cunt taste like?

ALICE. Heaven.

(Beat.)

LARRY. How long you been doing this?

ALICE. Three months.

LARRY. Straight after he left you?

ALICE. No one left me.

(Beat. Larry glances round the room.)

LARRY. Been here already tonight?

ALICE. Yes.

LARRY. With who?

ALICE. A couple. A man and a woman.

LARRY. What did you do?

ALICE. I stripped, I danced, I bent over.

LARRY. You gave this *couple* a thrill?

ALICE. I think so.

LARRY. What d'you talk about?

ALICE. This and that.

LARRY. D'you tell the truth?

ALICE. Yes and no.

LARRY. Are you telling *me* the truth?
ALICE. Yes.
LARRY. And no?
ALICE. I'm telling you the truth.
LARRY. Why?
ALICE. Because it's what you want.
LARRY. Yes. *It's what I want. (Larry stares at her.)* Nice *wig.*
ALICE. Thank you.
LARRY. Does it turn you on?
ALICE. Sometimes.
LARRY. *Liar.* You're telling me it turns you on because you think that's what I want to hear. You think *I'm* turned on by it turning *you* on.
ALICE. The thought of me *creaming* myself when I strip for strangers doesn't turn you on?
LARRY. Put like that ... yes. *(She shows him her behind.)* Are you flirting with me?
ALICE. Maybe.
LARRY. Are you *allowed* to flirt with me?
ALICE. Sure.
LARRY. Really?
ALICE. No I'm not, I'm breaking all the rules.
LARRY. You're mocking me. *(She sits opposite him.)*
ALICE. Yes, I'm allowed to flirt.
LARRY. To prise my money from me.
ALICE. To prise your money from you I can say or do as I please.
LARRY. Except *touch.*
ALICE. We are not allowed to touch.
LARRY. Is that a good rule do you think?
ALICE. Sometimes.
(Beat.)
LARRY. Open your legs. *(She does so.)*
Wider. *(She does so. Pause. Larry looks between her legs.)*
What would happen if I touched you now?
ALICE. I would call Security.
LARRY. And what would they do?

ALICE. They would ask you to leave and ask you not to come back.
LARRY. And if I refused to leave?
ALICE. They would remove you. This is a two-way mirror. *(She nods in the direction of the audience.)* There are cameras in the ceiling.
(Beat. Larry glances up and to the audience.)
LARRY. I think it's best that I don't attempt to touch you. *(He looks at her).*
I'd like to touch you ... *later.*
ALICE. I'm not a whore.
LARRY. I wouldn't pay. *(He gazes at her.)*
Why the fuck did he leave you?
(Beat.)
ALICE. What's your job?
LARRY. A question, you've asked me a question.
ALICE. So?
LARRY. It's a chink in your armour.
ALICE. I'm not wearing armour.
LARRY. *Yes you are.*
I'm in the skin trade.
ALICE. You own Strip Clubs?
LARRY. *(Smiles.)* Do I look like the sort of man who owns strip clubs?
ALICE. Yes. *(Larry looks in the mirror/audience.)*
LARRY. Define that look.
ALICE. *Rich.*
LARRY. Close your legs. I don't own Strip Clubs.
ALICE. Do you own Golf Clubs?
LARRY. You know what I do. *(Larry stands.)*
Why are you calling yourself Jane?
ALICE. Because it's my name.
LARRY. But we both know it isn't.
You're all protecting your identities. The girl in there who calls herself "Venus." What's her *real* name?
ALICE. Pluto.
LARRY. You're cheeky.

ALICE. Would you like me to stop being cheeky?

LARRY. No.

(Beat.)

ALICE. What's *your* name? *(Larry considers.)*

LARRY. Daniel.

(Beat.)

ALICE. Daniel the Dermatologist.

LARRY. I never told you my job.

ALICE. I guessed. *(Larry looks at her.)*

LARRY. *(Close.)* You're *strong.*

There's another one in there (judging by the scars, a recent patient of "Doctor Tit") she calls herself "Cupid." Who's going to tell her Cupid was a bloke?

ALICE. He wasn't a bloke, he was a little boy.

(Pause.)

LARRY. I'd like you to tell me your name. *Please. (He gives her £20.)*

ALICE. Thank you. My name is Jane.

LARRY. Your *real* name. *(He gives her £20.)*

ALICE. Thank you. My real name is Jane.

LARRY. Careful. *(He gives her £20.)*

ALICE. Thank you. It's still Jane.

LARRY. I've got another five hundred quid here. *(Larry takes out the money.)*

Why don't I give you — All — This — Money — and you tell me what your Real Name is, *(Larry raises her face towards his with the wad of notes.)* Alice. *(She tries to take the money. Larry withdraws it.)*

ALICE. I promise. *(Larry gives her the money.)* Thank you. My real name is Plain — Jane — Jones.

LARRY. I may be rich but I'm not stupid.

ALICE. What a shame "Doc," I love 'em rich and stupid.

LARRY. DON'T FUCK AROUND WITH ME.

ALICE. I apologise.

LARRY. *Accepted.* All the girls in this hellhole; the pneumatic robots, the coked-up baby dolls — and you're no different — you all use "stage names" to con yourselves you're someone else so you don't feel ashamed when you show your cunts and arse-holes to Complete Fucking Strangers.

I'm trying to have a conversation here.

ALICE. You're out of cash, Buster.

LARRY. I've paid for the room.

ALICE. This is extra.

(Pause.)

LARRY. We met last year.

ALICE. Wrong girl.

LARRY. I touched your face at Anna's ... opening.

I know you're in grief. I know you're ... "*destroyed.*"

TALK TO ME.

ALICE. I am.

LARRY. Talk to me in real life.

I didn't know you'd be here.

I know who you are.

I love your scar, I love everything about you that hurts.

(Silence. Larry slowly breaks down.)

She won't even see me ...

You feel the same, I *know* you feel the same.

ALICE. You can't cry here.

LARRY. Hold me, let me hold you. *(Larry approaches her.)*

ALICE. We're not allowed to touch.

(Pause.)

LARRY. Come home with me, Alice. It's *safe.* Let me look after you.

ALICE. I don't need looking after.

LARRY. *Everyone* needs looking after.

ALICE. I'm not your revenge fuck.

(Pause.)

LARRY. I'll pay you.

ALICE. I don't need your money.

LARRY. You *have* my money.

ALICE. Thank you.

LARRY. THANK YOU, THANK YOU. Is that some kind of rule?

ALICE. I'm just being polite.

(Pause. Larry sits down.)

LARRY. Get a lot of men in here, crying their guts out?

ALICE. Occupational hazard.

(Beat.)

LARRY. Have you ever desired a customer?

ALICE. Yes.

LARRY. Put me out of my misery, do you ... desire *me?* Because I'm being pretty fucking honest about my feelings for *you.*

ALICE. Your *"feelings"?*

LARRY. Whatever.

(Beat.)

ALICE. No. I don't desire you.

(Pause.)

LARRY. Thank you. Thank you sincerely for your honesty.

Next question: Do you think it's possible you could perceive me as something other than a sad slot machine spewing out money?

ALICE. That's the transaction; you're the customer, I'm the service.

LARRY. Hey, we're in a Strip Club let's not debate sexual politics.

ALICE. *Debate?*

LARRY. You're asking for a smack, gorgeous.

ALICE. No I'm not.

(Beat.)

LARRY. But you *are* gorgeous.

ALICE. "Thank you."

(Pause. Larry stands, straightens his tie, lights a cigarette.)

LARRY. Will you lend me my cab fare?

ALICE. *(Laughing.)* No.

LARRY. I'll give it back to you tomorrow ...

ALICE. Company policy, you give *us* the money.

LARRY. And what do we get in return?

ALICE. We're nice to you.

LARRY. "And We Get To See You Naked."

ALICE. It's beautiful.

LARRY. Except ... you think you haven't given us anything of yourselves.

You think because you don't love us or desire us or even like us you think you've *won*.

ALICE. It's not a war. *(Larry laughs for some time.)*

LARRY. But you do give us something of yourselves:

You give us ... *imagery* ... and we do with it what we will.

If you women could see one minute of our Home Movies — the shit that slops through our minds every day — you'd string us up by our balls, you really would.

You don't understand the territory.

Because you *are* the territory.

I could tell you to strip right now ...

ALICE. Yes. Do you want me to?

LARRY. No.

Alice ... tell me something *true*.

ALICE. Lying is the most fun a girl can have without taking her clothes off.

But it's better if you do.

LARRY. You're cold. You're all cold at heart. *(Larry stares into the two-way mirror.)*

WHAT D'YOU HAVE TO DO TO GET A BIT OF INTIMACY AROUND HERE?

ALICE. Well, maybe next time I'll have worked on my intimacy.

LARRY. No. I'll tell you what's going to work. What's going to *work* is that you're going to take your clothes off right now and you're going to turn around *very slowly* and bend over and touch the fucking floor for my viewing pleasure.

ALICE. That's what you want?

(Beat.)

LARRY. What else could I want? *(Alice looks straight at him and begins to undress, slowly.)*

BLACKOUT

Scene 8

Restaurant.

Evening/lunchtime. October. (A month later.)

Dan is sitting at a table with a drink. He is smoking. He waits. Anna joins him.

ANNA. Sorry, I'm really sorry. *(Dan kisses her.)*
DAN. What happened?
ANNA. Traffic. *(Anna sits.)*
DAN. You're flushed, you didn't need to run. *(Anna smiles.)*
ANNA. Have you ordered?
DAN. I ordered a menu about ten years ago.
(Pause. Dan looks at her.)
So ... how was it?
ANNA. Oh ... fine.
(Beat.)
DAN. You had lunch?
ANNA. Mm-hmm.
(Beat.)
DAN. Where?
(Beat.)
ANNA. Here, actually.
DAN. *Here?*
ANNA. He chose it.
DAN. Then what?
ANNA. Then we left.
(Pause.)
DAN. *And?*
ANNA. There is no "and."
DAN. You haven't seen him for four months, there must be an "and." *(Anna shrugs.)*
How is he?
ANNA. Terrible.

DAN. How's his *dermatology?*
ANNA. He is now in Private practice.
DAN. How does he square that with his politics?
ANNA. He's not much concerned with politics at present.
(Beat.)
DAN. Was he weeping all over the place?
ANNA. Some of the time.
DAN. *(Genuine.)* Poor bastard.
Was he ... "difficult"...?
ANNA. Are you angry I saw him?
DAN. No, no, it's just ... I haven't seen *Alice.*
ANNA. You can't see Alice, you don't know where she is.
DAN. I haven't tried to find her.
ANNA. He's been begging me to see him for months, you *know* why I saw him, I saw him so he'd ... *sign.*
DAN. So has he signed?
ANNA. *Yes.*
DAN. Congratulations. You are now a divorcée — double divorcée. Sorry. *(Dan takes her hand.)* How do you feel?
ANNA. Tired. *(Dan kisses her hand, Anna kisses his.)*
DAN. I love you. *And* ... I need a piss. *(Dan exits. Anna reaches into her bag and pulls out the divorce papers. Larry enters.)*
LARRY. *(Sitting.)* Afternoon.
ANNA. Hi. *(Larry looks around.)*
LARRY. I hate this place.
ANNA. At least it's central.
LARRY. I hate central. The centre of London's a theme park.
I hate "Retro" and I hate the future. Where does that leave me? *(He looks at her.)*
Come back.
ANNA. You promised you wouldn't.
LARRY. *Come back.*
(Beat.)
ANNA. How's work?
LARRY. Oh Jesus. Work's shit, OK.
(He looks around for a waiter. Loud.) Do they have waiters here?
ANNA. They're all busy.
LARRY. I love you. Please come back.

ANNA. I'm not coming back. *(Anna spreads the divorce papers on the table. Larry stares at them.)* Sign this, please.
LARRY. No pen. *(Anna hands him her pen.)*
ANNA. Pen. *(Larry takes her hand.)* Give me back my hand ... *(Larry lets go.)* Sign.
(Beat.)
LARRY. I'll sign it on one condition: we skip lunch, we go to my sleek, little surgery and we christen the patients' bed with our final fuck. I know you don't *want* to, I know you think I'm *sick* for asking — but that's what I'm asking — "For Old Time's Sake," because I'm obsessed with you, because I can't get over you unless you ... because I think on some small level you owe me *something*, for deceiving me so ... *exquisitely*.

For all these reasons I'm *begging* you to give me your body.

Be my whore and in return I will pay you with your liberty.

If you do this I swear I will not contact you again — you know I'm a man of my word.

I will divorce you and, in time, consider the possibility of a friendship. *(Larry stands.)*

I'm going to the bar. I assume you still drink vodka tonic? *(Anna nods. Larry exits. Dan returns and sits.)*
DAN. Any sign of a waiter?
ANNA. No.
DAN. Do you want some food?
ANNA. I'm not hungry. *(Dan stares at her, Anna turns to him, slowly.)*
DAN. You slept with him, didn't you?
(Pause.)
ANNA. Yes. I'm ... "sorry" ... *(Dan smiles.)*
DAN. What do you expect me to do?
ANNA. Understand ... hopefully?
(Beat.)
DAN. Why didn't you lie to me?
ANNA. We said we'd always tell each other the truth.
DAN. What's so great about the truth? Try lying for a change — it's the currency of the world.

ANNA. Dan, I did what he wanted and now he will leave us alone.

I love *you*, I didn't give *him* anything.

DAN. Your body? *(Dan reaches for his cigarettes.)*

ANNA. If Alice came to you ... *desperate* ... with all that love still between you and she said she needed you to want her so that she could get over you, you would do it.

I wouldn't like it either but I would forgive you because it's ... a mercy fuck — a *sympathy* fuck. Moral rape, everyone does it. It's ... *kindness.*

DAN. No, it's cowardice.

You don't have the guts to let him hate you.

Did you enjoy it?

ANNA. *No.*

DAN. So you hated every second of it? *(Anna looks at Dan.)*

Did you come?

ANNA. No.

DAN. Did you fake it?

ANNA. Yes.

DAN. Why?

ANNA. To make him *think* I enjoyed it, why do you think?

DAN. If you were just his *slag* why did you give him the pleasure of thinking you'd enjoyed it?

ANNA. I don't know, I just did.

DAN. You fake it with me?

ANNA. Yes, yes I do. I fake one in three, all right?

DAN. Tell me the truth.

(Pause.)

ANNA. *Occasionally* ... I have faked it.

It's not important, you don't *make* me come. I come ... you're ... "in the area" ... providing valiant assistance.

DAN. You make *me* come.

ANNA. You're a man, you'd come if the tooth fairy winked at you.

(Beat.)

DAN. You're late because you've come straight here from being with him.

(Beat.)

ANNA. Yes.

DAN. Where was it?

ANNA. His new surgery.

(Beat.)

DAN. Long session. *(Anna tries to touch him, he pulls away from her.)*

ANNA. Dan, please be bigger than ... *jealous.* Please, be bigger.

DAN. What could be bigger than jealousy?

(Long silence.)

ANNA. When we're making love, why don't you kiss me?

Why don't you like it when I say I love you?

I'm on your side. *Talk to me.*

DAN. It *hurts.* I'm ashamed. I know it's illogical and I do understand but *I hate you.*

I love you and I don't like other men fucking you, is that so weird?

ANNA. No. YES. It was only sex.

DAN. *(Hard.)* If you can still fuck him you haven't left him.

(Softly.) It's gone ... we're not innocent anymore.

ANNA. Don't stop loving me ... I can see it draining out of you.

I'm sorry, it was a stupid thing to do. It meant *nothing.*

If you love me enough you'll forgive me.

DAN. Are you *testing* me?

ANNA. *No.* Dan, I do understand.

DAN. *(Gently.)* No ... *he* understands. *(He looks at her.)*

All I can see is *him* all over you.

He's clever, your *ex*-husband ... I almost admire him.

(Silence.)

ANNA. Where are you?

Alice?

DAN. *(Smiles.)* I was reading the paper once. She wanted some attention. She crouched down on the carpet and pissed right in front of me.

Isn't that the most charming thing you've ever heard?

ANNA. *(Tough.)* Why did you swear eternal love when all you wanted was a fuck?

DAN. I didn't just want a fuck, I wanted you.

ANNA. You wanted excitement, love bores you.
DAN. No ... it disappoints me.
I think you enjoyed it; he wheedles you into bed, the old jokes, the strange familiarity, I think you had "a whale of a time" and the truth is, I'll never know unless I ask *him*.
ANNA. Well why don't you? *(Larry returns to the table with two drinks. Vodka tonic for Anna, Scotch and dry for himself.)*
LARRY. Vodka tonic for the lady.
ANNA. *(To Larry.)* Drink your drink and then we'll go. *(Larry looks at her. To Larry.)* I'm doing this because I feel guilty and because I pity you. You know that, don't you?
LARRY. Yes.
ANNA. *(To Larry.)* Feel good about yourself?
LARRY. No. *(Larry drinks.)*
DAN. *(To Anna.)* I'm sorry ...
ANNA. *(To Dan.)* I didn't do it to hurt you. It's not all about *you*.
DAN. *(To Anna.)* I know.
Let's go home ... *(Dan and Anna kiss.)*
I'll get us a cab. *(Dan exits. Larry sits.)*
LARRY. Will you tell him?
ANNA. I don't know.
LARRY. *(Helpful.)* Better to be truthful about this sort of thing ...
ANNA. Sign.
(Beat.)
LARRY. I forgive you.
ANNA. Sign. *(Larry signs.)*

BLACKOUT

Scene 9

Museum.

Afternoon. November. (A month later.)

A glass cabinet containing a life-size model of a Victorian child. A girl, dressed in rags. Behind her a model of a London street circa 1880s.

Alice is alone. She is wearing a cashmere sweater. She is looking at the exhibit. She is holding a small package.

Larry enters. He watches her.

LARRY. "Young Woman, London." *(Alice turns.)* Hallo, gorgeous.
ALICE. You're late, you old fart.
LARRY. Sorry. *(They kiss, warmly.)* You minx. *(Larry tugs the sweater.)*
ALICE. "The sacred sweater," I'll give it back.
LARRY. It suits you. Keep it.
ALICE. Thank you. *(Alice hands him the package.)* Happy Birthday.
LARRY. Thank you.
I'm late because I walked through Postman's Park to get here ... and I had a little look ... at the memorial.
ALICE. Oh.
LARRY. Yeah ... *oh. (Larry looks at the exhibit, smiles.)*
ALICE. Do you hate me?
LARRY. No, I adore you.
ALICE. Do we have to talk about it?
LARRY. Not if you don't want to. *(She kisses him.)*
ALICE. Thank you. I've got a surprise for you.
LARRY. You're full of them. *(Alice looks at Larry's watch.)*
ALICE. Wait here. *(Alice exits. Larry opens the package, looks inside, smiles. Anna enters, looking at her watch. She has a guidebook,*

camera and a large brown envelope. She is wearing the shoes Larry gave her in Scene 6. She sees Larry. Stops. Larry looks up, sees her.)

ANNA. What are *you* doing here?

LARRY. I'm ... lazing on a Sunday afternoon. You?

ANNA. I'm meeting Alice.

(Beat.)

LARRY. Who?

ANNA. Dan's Alice — Dan's ex-Alice. She phoned me at the studio this morning ... she wants her negatives ...

LARRY. ... Right ...

(Beat.)

ANNA. You don't go to museums.

LARRY. The evidence would suggest otherwise.

(Beat.)

ANNA. *(Suspicious.)* Are you OK?

LARRY. Yeah, you?

ANNA. Fine. It's your birthday today.

LARRY. I know.

(Beat.)

ANNA. I thought of you this morning.

LARRY. Lucky me.

(Beat.)

ANNA. Happy Birthday.

LARRY. Thank you. *(Anna nods to the package.)*

ANNA. Present?

LARRY. *(Evasive.) ... Yeah ...*

ANNA. What is it?

LARRY. A Newton's Cradle.

ANNA. Who from?

(Beat.)

LARRY. My dad.

ANNA. From *Joe?*

(Pause.)

LARRY. It's from *Alice.*

I'm fucking her.

I — Am — Fucking — Alice.

She's set us up, I had no idea you were meeting her.

(Pause.)

ANNA. You're old enough to be her ancestor.
LARRY. Disgusting, isn't it.
ANNA. You should be ashamed.
LARRY. *(Smiles.)* Oh, I am.
(Beat.)
ANNA. ... *How?*
LARRY. *(Vague.)* I went to a club, she happened to be there.
ANNA. A *club?*
LARRY. Yeah, a club.
ANNA. You don't go to clubs.
LARRY. I'm reliving my youth.
ANNA. Was it a strip club?
LARRY. You know, I can't remember. *(Larry looks at Anna.) Jealous? (Anna shrugs.)* Ah, well.
ANNA. When did it start?
LARRY. About a month ago.
ANNA. Before or after I came to your surgery?
LARRY. The night before. *(Dirty.)* She made me strip for her.
ANNA. I don't want to know.
LARRY. I know.
Did you tell your "soul mate" about *that* afternoon?
ANNA. Of course.
LARRY. How did he take it?
(Beat.)
ANNA. Like a man. *(She looks at him.)*
LARRY. I told you it was best to be truthful.
ANNA. You're sly.
LARRY. Am I?
(Fondly.) You love your guidebooks, you look like a tourist.
ANNA. I feel like one. Please don't hate me.
LARRY. It's easier than loving you. *(He looks at Anna.)*
Me and Alice ... it's *nothing.*
ANNA. Nice nothing?
LARRY. Very. *(They look at each other, close.)*
Since we're talking, could you have a word with your lawyer?
I'm still waiting for confirmation of our divorce.
If that's what you want. *(Alice enters.)*
ALICE. Hi, do you two know each other?

LARRY. I think I'll leave you to it.
ALICE. Good idea, we don't want *him* here while we're working, do we?
LARRY. *(To Alice.)* Later, Minx.
(To Anna.) Bye. *(He makes to exit, turns.)*
(To Anna.) Nice shoes by the way. *(Larry exits.)*
ANNA. How did you get so brutal?
ALICE. I lived a little. *(Alice strokes the sweater, Anna watches her.)*
ANNA. You're primitive.
ALICE. Yeah, I am. How's Dan?
ANNA. Fine.
ALICE. Did you tell him you were seeing me?
ANNA. No.
ALICE. Do you cut off his crusts?
ANNA. What?
ALICE. Do you cut off his crusts?
ANNA. What do you want?
ALICE. I want my negatives. *(Anna hands the envelope to Alice.)* What's your latest project, Anna?
ANNA. Derelict buildings.
ALICE. How nice, the beauty of ugliness.
ANNA. What are you doing with Larry?
ALICE. *Everything.*
I like your bed.
You should come round one night, come and watch your husband blubbering into his pillow — it might help you develop a conscience.
ANNA. I know what I've done.
ALICE. His big thing at the moment is how upset his family are. Apparently, they all worship you, they can't understand why you had to ruin everything. He spends *hours* staring up my arsehole like there's going to be some answer there.
Any ideas, Anna?
Why don't you go back to him?
ANNA. And then Dan would go back to you?
ALICE. Maybe.
ANNA. *Ask* him.
ALICE. I'm not a beggar.

ANNA. Dan left you, I didn't force him to go.
ALICE. You made yourself available, don't weasel out of it.
ANNA. Screwing Larry was a big mistake.
ALICE. Yeah, well, *everyone* screws Larry round here.
ANNA. You're Dan's little girl, he won't like it.
ALICE. So don't tell him, I think you owe me that. *(Anna looks away.)* She even looks beautiful when she's angry. The Perfect Woman.
ANNA. JUST FUCKING STOP IT.
ALICE. Now we're talking.
ANNA. Why *now*, why come for me *now?*
ALICE. Because I felt strong enough, it's taken me five months to convince myself you're not better than me.
ANNA. It's not a competition.
ALICE. Yes it is.
ANNA. I don't want a fight.
ALICE. SO GIVE IN.
(Silence. They look at each other. Gently.) Why did you do this?
ANNA. *(Tough.)* I fell in love with him, Alice.
ALICE. That's the most stupid expression in the world.
"I fell in love" — as if you had no *choice.*
There's a moment, there's always a *moment;* I can do this, I can give in to this or I can resist it. I don't know when your moment was but I bet there was one.
ANNA. Yes, there was.
ALICE. You didn't fall in love, you gave in to temptation.
ANNA. Well *you* fell in love with him.
ALICE. No, I *chose* him. I looked in his briefcase and I found this ... *sandwich* ... and I thought, "I will give all my love to this charming man who cuts off his crusts."
I didn't *fall* in love, I chose to.
ANNA. You still want him, after everything he's done to you?
ALICE. You wouldn't understand, he ... *buries* me.
He makes me invisible.
ANNA. *(Curious.)* What are you *hiding* from?
ALICE. *(Softly.)* Everything. Everything's a lie, nothing matters.
ANNA. Too easy, Alice. It's the cop-out of the age.

ALICE. Yeah well, you're *old.* *(Anna smiles to herself, looks at Alice.)*
ANNA. I am sorry. I had a choice and I chose to be selfish. I'm sorry.
ALICE. *(Shrugs.)* Everyone's selfish, I stole Dan from someone else.
ANNA. *Ruth?*
ALICE. Ruth. She went to pieces when he left her.
ANNA. Did *she* ever come and see *you?*
ALICE. No. *(Alice turns to Anna.) So* ... what are you going to do?
ANNA. *Think. (Anna touches Alice's sweater.)*
Is Larry nice to you, in bed?
ALICE. OK, Dan's better.
ANNA. Rubbish, at least Larry's *there.*
ALICE. Dan's there, in his own quiet way.
ANNA. They spend a lifetime fucking and never know how to make love.
(Pause.)
ALICE. I've got a scar on my leg, Larry's mad about it, he licks it like a dog. Any ideas?
ANNA. *(Shrugs.) Dermatology?* God knows. This is what we're dealing with.
We arrive with our ... "baggage" and for a while they're brilliant, they're "Baggage Handlers."
We say, "Where's *your* baggage?" They deny all knowledge of it ... *"They're in love"* ... they have none.
Then ... just as you're relaxing ... a Great Big Juggernaut arrives ... with *their* baggage.
It Got Held Up.
One of the greatest myths men have about women is that we overpack.
They love the way we make them *feel* but not "us."
They love dreams.
ALICE. So do we. You should lower your expectations.
ANNA. It's easy to say that. I'm not being patronising but you're a child.
ALICE. You are being patronising.

ANNA. And you *are* a child. *(They look at each other.)*
Who's "*Buster*"?
ALICE. "Buster"? No idea.
ANNA. He says it in his sleep.
ALICE. *(Smiles.)* I've got to go. *(Alice makes to exit.)*
ANNA. Don't forget your negatives. *(Alice picks up the envelope.)*
ALICE. Oh, yeah. Thanks. *(Alice hands the envelope to Anna.)*
Do the right thing, Anna. *(Alice exits. Anna looks at the envelope.)*

BLACKOUT

Scene 10

Larry's surgery.

Late afternoon. December. (A month later.)

On Larry's desk: computer, phone, a Newton's Cradle. Also in the room, a surgery bed. Larry is seated at his desk.

Dan is standing, distraught. He holds his brown briefcase.

Silence.

LARRY. So?
DAN. I want Anna back.
LARRY. She's made her choice.
You look like *shit.*
(Beat. Dan puts his briefcase down.)
DAN. I owe you an apology. I fell in love with her.
My intention was not to make you suffer.
LARRY. Where's the apology? You cunt.

DAN. I apologise.

If you love her, you'll let her go so she can be ... happy.

LARRY. She doesn't want to be "happy."

DAN. Everyone wants to be happy.

LARRY. Depressives don't. They want to be *unhappy* to confirm they're depressed.

If they were happy they couldn't be depressed anymore, they'd have to go out into the world and *live*, which can be ... *depressing.*

DAN. Anna's not a depressive.

LARRY. Isn't she?

DAN. I love her.

LARRY. Boo hoo, so do I. You don't love Anna, you love yourself.

DAN. You're *wrong*, I don't love myself.

LARRY. Yes you do, and you know something; you're *winning* — you selfish people — it's *your* world. *Nice*, isn't it? *(Dan glances round the sleek surgery.)*

DAN. *Nice* office.

It's *you* who's selfish. You don't even want *Anna*, you want revenge.

She's gone back to you because she can't bear your *suffering.*

You don't know who she is, you love her like a dog loves its owner.

LARRY. And the owner loves the dog for so doing.

Companionship will always triumph over "*passion.*"

DAN. You'll hurt her, you'll never forgive her.

LARRY. Of course I'll forgive her — I *have* forgiven her.

Without forgiveness we're savages. You're *drowning.*

DAN. You only *met* her because of me.

LARRY. Yeah ... *thanks.*

DAN. It's a joke, your marriage to her is a joke.

LARRY. Here's a good one: she never sent the divorce papers to her lawyer.

To a "Towering Romantic Hero" like you I don't doubt I'm somewhat common but I am, nevertheless, what she has chosen.

And we must respect What The Woman Wants.

If you go *near* her again, I promise — *(The phone rings.)* I will kill you. *(Larry picks it up. In phone.)* Uh-huh. OK. *(Larry puts the phone down.)*

I have patients to see. *(Larry takes his jacket off to prepare for his patient.)*

DAN. When she came here you think she enjoyed it?

LARRY. I didn't fuck her to give her a "*nice time.*"

I fucked her to fuck you up. A good fight is never clean.

And yeah, she enjoyed it, she's a Catholic — she loves a guilty fuck. *(Larry grins.)*

DAN. You're an animal.

LARRY. YES. What are *you?*

DAN. You think love is simple? You think the heart is like a diagram?

LARRY. Ever *seen* a human heart? It looks like a fist wrapped in blood.

GO FUCK YOURSELF ... you ... *WRITER*. You LIAR.

Go check a few facts while I get my hands dirty.

DAN. She hates your hands. She hates your simplicity.

(Pause.)

LARRY. Listen ... I've spent the whole week talking about *you.*

Anna tells me you fucked her with your eyes closed.

She tells me you wake in the night, crying for your dead mother.

You mummy's boy.

Shall we stop this?

It's *over.* Accept it.

You don't know the first thing about love because you don't understand *compromise.*

You don't even know ... *Alice. (Dan looks at him.)*

Consider her scar, how did she get that?

(Beat.)

DAN. When did *you* meet Alice?

(Pause.)

LARRY. Anna's exhibition. *You* remember.

A scar in the shape of a question mark, solve the mystery.

DAN. She got it when her parents' car crashed.

(Pause.)

LARRY. There's a condition called *"Dermatitis Artefacta."* It's a mental disorder manifested in the skin. The patient manufactures his or her very own skin disease. They pour bleach on themselves, gouge their skin, inject themselves with their own piss, sometimes their own shit. They create their own disease with the same diabolical attention to detail as the artist or the lover. It looks "real" but its source is the deluded self. *(Larry takes a roll of paper and makes a new sheet on the surgery bed.)*

I think Alice mutilated herself.

It's fairly common in children who lose their parents young.

They blame themselves, they're disturbed.

DAN. Alice is not "disturbed."

LARRY. But she *is*.

You were so busy feeling your grand artistic *"feelings"* you couldn't see what was in front of you. The girl is fragile and tender. She didn't want to be put in a book, she wanted to be *loved*.

DAN. How do *you* know?

(Beat.)

LARRY. Clinical observation. *(Larry hands Dan his briefcase indicating for him to leave. Larry looks at Dan, close.)*

Don't cry on me.

(Silence. Dan breaks down, uncontrollably. Larry observes him.)

DAN. I'm sorry. *(He continues to cry.)*

I don't know what to do. *(Larry watches him sob. Eventually ...)*

LARRY. Sit down. *(Dan sinks into a chair, head in hands.)*

You want my advice? Go back to her.

DAN. She'd never have me. She's vanished.

(Pause.)

LARRY. No, she hasn't. *(Dan looks up.)*

I found her ... by accident. She's working in ... a ... "club."

Yes, I saw her naked.

No, I did not fuck her.

DAN. You spoke to her?

LARRY. Yes.

DAN. What about?

LARRY. *You.* (*The phone rings. Larry picks it up. He hands Dan a Kleenex. In phone.*) Yes. One minute. *(Larry puts the phone down. He writes on his prescription pad.)*

DAN. How is she?

LARRY. *(Writing.)* She loves you. Beyond Comprehension.

Here ... your prescription. *(Larry hands Dan a piece of paper.)* It's where she works.

Go to her. *(They look at each other.)*

DAN. Thank you. *(Larry starts to consult his files. Dan moves to leave but then gestures to the Newton's Cradle.)*

Where did you get that?

LARRY. A present. (*Larry begins to work on his computer.)*

Still pissing about on the Net?

DAN. Not recently.

(Beat.)

LARRY. I wanted to *kill* you.

DAN. I thought you wanted to *fuck* me.

LARRY. *(Smiles.)* Don't get lippy.

I liked your book by the way.

DAN. Thanks ... You Stand Alone.

LARRY. *With Anna.* I'm not sucking your literary cock but I did quite like it — because it was "humane" (surprisingly). You should write another one.

DAN. *(Shrugs.)* Haven't got a subject.

(Beat.)

LARRY. When I was nine, a policeman touched me up.

He was my uncle. Still *is.* Uncle Ted.

Nice bloke, married, bit of a demon darts player.

Don't tell me you haven't got a subject, every human life is a million stories.

Thank God life *ends* — we'd never survive it.

From Big Bang to weary shag, the history of the world.

Our flesh is ferocious ... our bodies will kill us ... our bones will outlive us.

Still writing obituaries?

DAN. Yes.

LARRY. Busy?

DAN. *(Nods.)* I was made editor.

LARRY. Yeah? How come?

DAN. The previous editor died. *(They smile.)*
Alcohol poisoning. I sat with him for a week, in the hospital. *(They look at each other.)*

LARRY. I really do have patients to see. *(Dan gestures to the Newton's Cradle.)*

DAN. Alice ... gave me one of those.

LARRY. Really?

(Beat.)

DAN. And yours?

LARRY. My dad.

DAN. *(Suspicious.)* Your father?

LARRY. Yeah, he loves old tat.

DAN. He's a cabdriver, isn't he?

LARRY. Yeah. *(Larry points to Dan indicating, "and yours.")*
... Teacher?

DAN. History.

(Pause. Larry sets the cradle in motion. They watch it moving.)

LARRY. You should never have messed with Anna. *(Dan gets up.)*

DAN. I know, I'm sorry. Thank you.

LARRY. For what?

DAN. Being kind.

LARRY. I am kind. Your invoice is in the post. *(Dan goes to exit.)*
Dan ... *(Dan turns to Larry.)*
I lied to you.
I did fuck Alice.
I'm sorry for telling you.
I'm just ... not ... *big enough* to forgive you.
Buster. *(They look at each other.)*

BLACKOUT

Scene 11

Hotel room.

Late night. January. (A month later.)

Dan is lying on the bed, smoking. He is reading a Gideon's Bible. He stubs his cigarette in the ashtray.

Alice is in the bathroom offstage.

ALICE. *(Off.)* SHOW ME THE SNEER. *(Dan sneers in the direction of the bathroom.)*
(Off.) BOLLOCKS.
DAN. *(Laughing.)* It's two in the morning, you'll wake the hotel. *(Alice enters in her pyjamas. She cartwheels onto the bed.)*
ALICE. Fuck me.
DAN. *Again?* We have to be up at six.
ALICE. How can *one* man be so endlessly disappointing?
DAN. That's my *charm. (Alice lies in his arms.)* So ... where are we going?
ALICE. My treat — my holiday surprise — my rules. *(Dan tickles her.)*
DAN. *Where* are we *going?*
ALICE. *(Laughing.)* New York.
DAN. You angel.
How long's the flight?
ALICE. Seven hours.
DAN. I can't fly for seven hours.
ALICE. The *plane* will do the flying. I'll protect you. *(She kisses him.)*
Don't be scared of flying.
DAN. I'm not, I'm scared of *crashing.* Did you remember to pack my passport?
ALICE. Of course, it's with my passport.
DAN. And where's that?

ALICE. In a place where *you* can't look. *No one* sees my passport photo. *(Dan strokes her.)*

Hey, when we get on the plane we'll have been together four years.

Happy Anniversary ... *Buster. (Dan stops, looks at her.)*

DAN. I'm going to take my eyes out.

ALICE. Brush your teeth as well. *(Dan gets off the bed.)*

DAN. What was in my sandwiches?

ALICE. Tuna.

DAN. What colour was my apple?

ALICE. Green.

DAN. It was *red.*

ALICE. It was *green* and it was horrible.

DAN. What were your first words to me?

ALICE. "Hallo, Stranger."

DAN. What a slut.

(Beat.)

ALICE. Where had I been?

DAN. "Clubbing," then the meat market and then ... the buried river.

(Beat.)

ALICE. The what?

DAN. You went to Blackfriars Bridge to see where the Fleet river comes out ... *the swimming pig* ... all that.

ALICE. You've lost the plot, *Grandad. (Dan "remembers" and exits to the bathroom.)*

DAN. *(Off.)* And you went to that *park* ... with the memorial.

ALICE. Who did *you* go there with?

DAN. *(Off.)* My old dead dad.

ALICE. He ate an egg sandwich, he had butter on his chin.

DAN. *(Off.)* How do you *remember* these things?

ALICE. Because *my* head's not full of specky, egghead rubbish.

What was your euphemism?

DAN. *(Off.)* Reserved. Yours?

ALICE. Disarming. Were the chairs red or yellow? *(Dan enters. He is now wearing his spectacles.)*

DAN. No idea.

ALICE. Trick question, they were orange.

DAN. *You* are a trick question. *Damsel.*

ALICE. *Knight. (Alice opens her legs. Dan looks at her, remembers something. Pause.)*

DAN. Do you remember a doctor?

(Beat.)

ALICE. No ... what doctor?

(Pause.)

DAN. There was a *doctor* ... he gave you a cigarette.

(Beat.)

ALICE. No. I haven't been on holiday for ... *ever.*

DAN. We went to the country.

ALICE. That doesn't count, you were making sneaky calls to that ... *witch* we do not mention. *(Dan watches her.)*

DAN. Do you think they're happy?

ALICE. Who?

DAN. Anna and ... *Larry.*

ALICE. Couldn't give a toss. Come to bed.

DAN. I want a *fag.* How did *you* manage to give up?

ALICE. Deep Inner Strength. *(Dan gets into bed. He holds Alice, kisses her, strokes her leg.)*

DAN. How *did* you get this?

ALICE. You know how.

DAN. How?

ALICE. I fell off my bike because I refused to use stabilisers.

DAN. *(Disbelieving.)* Really?

ALICE. You know how I got it.

(Beat.)

DAN. Did you do it yourself?

ALICE. No.

(Beat.)

DAN. Show me your passport.

ALICE. No, I look ugly.

(Beat.)

DAN. When are you going to stop stripping?

ALICE. Soon.

DAN. You're *addicted* to it.

ALICE. No I'm not.

It paid for this.

(Pause. Dan struggles but can't stop himself.)

DAN. Tell me what happened.

ALICE. Dan ... *don't.* Nothing happened.

DAN. But he came to the club?

ALICE. Loads of men came to the club. *You* came to the club.

The look on your face.

DAN. The look on *your* face.

What a face. What a *wig. (He gazes at her.)*

I *love* your face ... I saw *this* face ... this ... *vision.*

And then you stepped into the road.

It was the moment of my life.

ALICE. *This* is the moment of your life.

DAN. You were perfect.

ALICE. I still am.

DAN. I know.

On the way to the hospital ... when you were "*lolling*" ... I kissed your forehead.

ALICE. You brute!

DAN. The cabbie saw me kiss you ... he said, "Is she yours?" and I said, "Yes ... she's *mine.*" *(Dan kisses her forehead, holds her close. Struggles with himself.)*

So he came to the club, watched you strip, had a little chat and that was it?

ALICE. Yes.

DAN. You're not *trusting* me. I'm in love with you, you're *safe.*

If you fucked him you fucked him, I just want to know.

ALICE. Why?

DAN. *(Tenderly.)* Because I want to know *everything* because ... I'm ... *insane. (Dan strokes her face.)*

(Pause.)

Tell me ...

(Long silence.)

ALICE. Nothing happened. You were living with someone else.

DAN. *(Sharp.)* What are you justifying?

ALICE. I'm not justifying anything ... I'm just *saying.*

DAN. What are you saying?

ALICE. I'm not saying anything.

DAN. I just want the truth. *(Dan gets out of bed and puts his trousers on.)*

ALICE. I'm telling you the truth.

DAN. You and the truth are known strangers.

Did you ever give him a present?

(Beat.)

ALICE. No. Where are you going?

DAN. Cigarettes.

ALICE. Everywhere's closed.

DAN. I'll go to the terminal, I'll be back soon. *(Dan puts his coat on.)*

When I get back *please* tell me the truth.

ALICE. Why?

DAN. Because I'm addicted to it. Because without it we're animals. Trust me, I love you. *(He looks at her.)*

What? *(Alice slowly turns to him.)*

(Silence.)

ALICE. I don't love you anymore.

(Pause.)

DAN. Look ... I'm sorry ...

ALICE. No, I've changed the subject. I don't love you anymore.

DAN. Since when?

ALICE. *(Gently.)* Now ... Just Now.

I don't want to lie and I can't tell the truth so it's over.

DAN. Alice ... don't leave me. *(Alice gets out of bed and goes to her rucksack, she finds Dan's passport and hands it to him.)*

ALICE. I've left ... I've *gone.*

"I don't love you anymore. Good-bye."

(Beat.)

DAN. Why don't you tell me the truth?

ALICE. *(Softly.)* So you can hate me?

I fucked Larry. Many times. I enjoyed it. I came. I prefer *you.* Now go.

(Pause.)

DAN. I knew that, he told me.

ALICE. You *knew?*

DAN. I needed *you* to tell me.

ALICE. *Why?*

DAN. Because he might've been lying, I had to hear it from *you.*

ALICE. I would never have told you because I know you'd never forgive me.

DAN. I would, I *have.*

ALICE. Why did he tell you?

DAN. Because he's a bastard.

ALICE. *(Distraught.)* How could he?

DAN. Because he wanted this to happen.

ALICE. But why *test* me?

DAN. Because I'm an idiot.

ALICE. *Yeah.*

I would've loved you forever. Now, please go.

DAN. Don't do this Alice, talk to me.

ALICE. I'm talking — *fuck off.*

DAN. I'm sorry, you misunderstand, I didn't mean to —

ALICE. Yes you did.

DAN. *I love you.*

ALICE. *Where?*

DAN. What?

ALICE. *Show me.* Where is this *"love"?*

I can't see it, I can't *touch* it, I can't *feel* it.

I can hear it, I can hear some *words* but I can't *do* anything with your easy words.

DAN. Listen to me, please —

ALICE. Whatever you say it's too late.

DAN. *(Desperately.) Please* don't do this.

ALICE. It's done. Now go or I'll call ... *security.*

(Beat.)

DAN. You're not in a strip club. There is no security. *(They look at each other. Pause. Alice tries to grab the phone. Dan throws her onto the bed. They struggle.)*

DAN. Why'd you fuck him?

ALICE. I wanted to.

DAN. *Why?*

ALICE. I *desired* him.

DAN. *Why?*

ALICE. *You* weren't there.
DAN. Why him?
ALICE. He asked me nicely.
DAN. You're a liar.
ALICE. So?
DAN. WHO ARE YOU?
ALICE. I'M NO ONE. *(She spits in his face. He grabs her by the throat, one hand.)*
Go on, hit me. That's what you *want*. Hit me, you fucker.
(Silence. Dan hits Alice. Silence.)
ALICE. Do you have a single original thought in your head?

BLACKOUT

Scene 12

Postman's Park.

Afternoon. July. (Six months later.)

A summer's day. Anna is looking at the memorial. She has a guidebook.

Larry stands, holding his white coat. He carries two Styrofoam cups. He watches her. She turns.

ANNA. *Spy. (Larry approaches.)* You've got the coat.
LARRY. The white coat.
ANNA. Hallo, Doctor Larry. *(Larry hands a cup to Anna.)*
Thanks. Have you read these? *(Anna turns back to the memorial.)*
LARRY. Yeah, I knew you'd like it. *(Larry sits on a park bench and lights a cigarette.)*
ANNA. *(Reading.)* Elizabeth Boxall ... aged seventeen ... who

died of injuries received in trying to save a child from a runaway horse. June 20TH 1888. *(Anna turns to Larry.)*

How's Polly?

(Beat.)

LARRY. Polly's great.

ANNA. I always knew you'd end up with a pretty nurse.

LARRY. Yeah? How?

ANNA. I just thought you would.

Is she ... "the one"?

LARRY. I don't know. *(He glances at Anna.)*

No.

Everyone learns, nobody changes.

ANNA. *You* don't change.

(Beat.)

LARRY. You ... seeing anyone?

ANNA. No.

I got a dog.

LARRY. Yeah? What sort?

ANNA. Mongrel, she's a stray. I found her in the street, no collar ... nothing.

(Pause.)

LARRY. You look fantastic.

ANNA. Don't *start.*

LARRY. I'd give you one ... *(Anna looks at him.)*

Serious.

ANNA. Fuck off and die, you fucked-up slag.

(Pause.)

LARRY. I never told you this: when I strode into the bathroom ... *that night* ... I banged my knee on our cast-iron tub. The bathroom *ambushed* me. While you were sobbing in the sitting room I was hopping around in agony. The mirror was having a field day. *(Anna smiles.)*

How's work?

ANNA. I'm having a break ... I'm taking the dog to the country ... we're going to go for long walks.

(Beat.)

LARRY. Don't become ... a sad person.

ANNA. I won't. I'm *not.* Fuck off. *(Larry looks at her.)*

LARRY. Don't give your love to a dog.
ANNA. Well, *you* didn't want it, in the end.
There's always someone younger. *(They look out at the memorial.)* *(Silence.)*
LARRY. How did she die?
ANNA. I don't know. When he phoned, he said it happened last night in New York. He's flying out today and he wanted to see us before he left.
LARRY. So they weren't together?
ANNA. They split up in January.
(Beat.)
LARRY. Did he say why?
ANNA. No.
(Beat.)
LARRY. How did they contact him?
ANNA. Maybe she wrote his name in her passport as "next of kin."
You're still in mine — "in the event of death."
I must remove you.
Are you glad you're back at the hospital? *(Anna sits with Larry.)*
LARRY. Yeah. Well, Polly said she wouldn't have sex with me until I gave up private medicine. What's a man to do? *(Anna looks at the memorial.)*
ANNA. Do you think the families arranged these?
LARRY. I suppose. It's like putting flowers at the roadside. People need to remember. It makes things seem less ... random.
Actually, I hate this memorial.
ANNA. Why?
LARRY. It's the sentimental act of a Victorian philanthropist: remember the dead, forget the living.
ANNA. You're a pompous bastard.
LARRY. And *you* are an incurable romantic.
Have a look for Alice Ayres.
ANNA. Larry, that's horrible. *(Larry points to one memorial in particular.)*
LARRY. *(Reading.)* Alice Ayres, daughter of a bricklayer's labourer, who by intrepid conduct saved three children from a

burning house in Union Street, Borough, at the cost of her own young life.

April 24TH 1885.

She made herself up. *(They look at the memorial. After a while, Larry puts his cigarette out and picks up his white coat.)*

I'm not being callous but I've got a lot of patients to see.

Will you give my apologies to Dan? I'm not good at grief.

ANNA. You're a coward.

LARRY. I know. *(Anna continues to look at the memorial then turns to Larry.)*

ANNA. You do remember me? *(They look at each other. Dan enters. He is wearing the suit and carrying the suitcase seen in Scene 5. He is holding a bunch of flowers. He is exhausted.)*

DAN. I couldn't get away from work, sorry.

LARRY. Dan ... I'm sorry ... I have to ...

DAN. It's fine. *(Larry exits.)*

DAN. *(To Anna.)* You look well.

ANNA. I am well. *(Dan looks out at the memorial.)*

ANNA. Dan ... *(Anna gestures for him to sit, he remains standing.)*

DAN. This is where we sat.

ANNA. Who?

DAN. Me and my father, didn't I tell you?

ANNA. No, wrong girl, you told Alice.

(Beat.)

DAN. *Jane.* Her name was Jane Jones.

The police phoned me ... they said that someone I knew, called Jane, had died ... (they found her address book). I said there must be a mistake ...

They had to *describe* her.

There's no one else to identify the body.

She was knocked down by a car ... on 43RD and Madison.

When I went to work today ... Graham said, "Who's on the slab?"

I went out to the fire escape and just ... cried like a baby.

I covered my face — why do we do that?

A man from the Treasury had died. I spent all morning ... writing his obituary.

There's no space. There's not enough ... *space. (Dan sits on the bench with Anna.)*

The phone rang. It was the police ... they said there's no record of her parents' death ... they said they were trying to trace them.

She told me that she fell in love with me because ... I cut off my crusts ... but it was just ... it was only *that* day ... because the bread ... *broke* in my hands. *(Dan turns away from Anna, looks at the flowers.)*

(Silence.)

(He turns back to Anna.)

I bumped into *Ruth* last week.

She's married. One kid, another on the way.

She married ... a Spanish *poet. (He grimaces.)*

She translated his work and fell in love with him.

Fell in love with a collection of poems.

They were called ... *Solitude. (Dan holds onto the flowers.)*

I have to put these at Blackfriars Bridge. *(Dan and Anna stand.)*

I have to go, I'll miss the plane. *(They look at each other.)*

Good-bye.

ANNA. Yes. Good-bye. *(They exit separately. Empty stage.)*

BLACKOUT

APPENDIX TO SCENE 3

In a production of *Closer* where budget or theatre sight lines won't allow for a projected version of this scene it may be possible for the actors to speak their lines whilst "typing." Permission, in this respect, must be sought from the author's agent when applying for the rights for the production.

The following dialogue may be used:

Scene 3

Internet.

Early evening. January. (The following year.)

Dan is in his flat sitting at a table with a computer. There is a Newton's Cradle on the table. Writerly sloth, etc.

Larry is sitting at his hospital desk with a computer. He is wearing a white coat.

They are in separate rooms.

They speak their "dialogue" simultaneous to their typing it. The actors should speak word by word, almost robotically, as if they were dictating the words onto the screen. Thus making a distinction between "typed" speech and "spoken" speech (e.g. Larry on the phone).

DAN. Hallo.
LARRY. Hi.

DAN. How are you?
LARRY. OK.
DAN. Come here often?
LARRY. Eh?
DAN. Net.
LARRY. First time.
DAN. A Virgin. Welcome. What's your name?
LARRY. Larry. You? *(Dan considers.)*
DAN. Anna.
LARRY. Nice to meet you.
DAN. I love COCK.
(Pause.)
LARRY. You're very forward.
DAN. And you are chatting on "LONDON FUCK." Do you want sex?
LARRY. Yes. Describe you.
DAN. Dark hair. Dirty mouth. Epic Tits.
LARRY. Define Epic.
DAN. 36DD.
LARRY. Nice arse?
DAN. Y.
LARRY. Because I want to know. *(Dan smiles.)*
DAN. No, "Y" means "Yes."
LARRY. Oh.
DAN. I want to suck you senseless.
LARRY. Be my guest.
DAN. Sit on my face Fuckboy.
LARRY. I'm there.
DAN. Wear my wet knickers.
(Beat.)
LARRY. OK.
DAN. Are you well hung?
LARRY. Nine pounds.
(Speaking.) Shit.
(Typing.) Nine inches.
DAN. GET IT OUT. *(Larry considers and then unzips. He puts his hand in his trousers. The phone on his desk rings. Loud. He jumps.)*
LARRY. *(Speaking.)* Wait.

(Typing.) Wait. *(Larry picks up the phone. Dan lights a cigarette.)*

(Speaking.) Yes. What's the histology? *Progressive?* Sounds like an atrophy. *(Larry puts the phone down and goes back to his keyboard. Dan clicks the balls on his Newton's Cradle.)*

Hallo? *(Dan looks at his screen.)*

Anna.

(Speaking.) Bollocks.

(Typing.) ANNA? WHERE ARE YOU?

DAN. Hey, big Larry, what do you wank about? *(Larry considers.)*

LARRY. Ex-girlfriends.

DAN. Not current g-friends?

LARRY. Never. *(Dan smiles.)*

DAN. Tell me your sex-ex fantasy ...

LARRY. Hotel room ... they tie me up ... tease me ... won't let me come. They fight over me, six tongues on my cock, balls, perineum, et cetera.

DAN. All hail the Sultan of Twat? *(Larry laughs.)*

LARRY. Anna, what do you wank about? *(Dan thinks.)*

DAN. Strangers.

LARRY. Details.

DAN. They form a queue and I attend to them like a cum hungry bitch, one in each hole and both hands.

LARRY. Then?

DAN. They come in my mouth arse tits cunt hair.

LARRY. *(Speaking.)* Jesus. *(Larry's phone rings. He picks up the receiver and replaces it without answering. Then he takes it off the hook.)*

(Typing.) Then?

DAN. I lick it off like the dirty slut I am. Wait, have to type with one hand ...

I'm coming right now ... oh oh oh oh oh oh oh oh oh oh oh oh oh oh oh.

(Pause. Larry, motionless, stares at his screen.)

LARRY. Was it good?

DAN. No. *(Larry shakes his head.)*

LARRY. I'm shocked.

DAN. PARADISE SHOULD BE SHOCKING.

LARRY. Are you for real?

(Beat.)
DAN. MEET ME.
(Pause.)
LARRY. Serious?
DAN. Y.
LARRY. When
DAN. NOW.
LARRY. Can't. I'm a Doctor. Must do rounds. *(Dan smiles. Larry flicks through his desk diary.)*
DAN. Don't be a pussy. Life without risk is death. Desire, like the world, is an accident. The best sex is anonymous. We live as we dream, ALONE. I'll make you come like a train.
LARRY. Tomorrow, 1P.M., where? *(Dan thinks.)*
DAN. The Aquarium, London Zoo and then HOTEL.
LARRY. How will you know me?
DAN. Bring white coat.
LARRY. Eh?
DAN. Doctor plus coat equals horn for me.
LARRY. OK.
DAN. I send you a rose my love.
LARRY. Thanks. See you at Aquarium. Bye Anna.
DAN. Bye Larry, kiss kiss kiss kiss kiss.
LARRY. Kiss kiss kiss kiss kiss kiss. *(They look at their screens.)*

BLACKOUT

PROPERTY LIST

Cigarettes, lighter and/or matches

Rucksack (ALICE)
Brown leather briefcase (DAN)
Stage blood (ALICE)
Strands of wool (ALICE)
Sandwiches wrapped in silver foil (ALICE)
Green and red apples (ALICE)
Two hot drinks in Styrofoam cups (DAN)
Watches (DAN, LARRY)
Mobile phone (DAN)
Camera (ANNA)
Light for photography (ANNA)
Light meter (ANNA)
Camera case (ANNA)
Computers (DAN, LARRY)
Phone (LARRY)
Newton's Cradle (DAN)
Desk diary (LARRY)
Three guidebooks (ANNA):
  London Zoo guidebook
  Museum guidebook
  Postman's Park guidebook
Crumpled rose (LARRY)
Bottle of lager (ALICE)
Glass of wine (DAN)
Bottle of wine (LARRY)
Glass (LARRY)
Small suitcase (DAN)
Suitcase (LARRY)
Bags (LARRY)
Jacket (LARRY)
Bottle of Scotch (LARRY)
Shoe box with shoes in it (LARRY)
Postcard (LARRY)

Two cups of tea (DAN)
Twenty-pound bills (LARRY)
Drinks (LARRY, DAN)
Bag (ANNA)
Divorce papers (ANNA)
Pen (ANNA)
Small package (ALICE)
Large brown envelope (ANNA)
Roll of paper for surgery bed (LARRY)
Kleenex (LARRY)
Prescription pad (LARRY)
Files (LARRY)
Gideon's Bible (DAN)
Ashtray (DAN)
Spectacles (DAN)
Trousers (DAN)
Coat (DAN)
Passport (ALICE)
White coat (LARRY)
Two Styrofoam cups (LARRY)
Bunch of flowers (DAN)

SOUND EFFECTS

Door buzzer
Phone ring

NEW PLAYS

★ **THE GREAT AMERICAN TRAILER PARK MUSICAL music and lyrics by David Nehls, book by Betsy Kelso.** Pippi, a stripper on the run, has just moved into Armadillo Acres, wreaking havoc among the tenants of Florida's most exclusive trailer park. "Adultery, strippers, murderous ex-boyfriends, Costco and the Ice Capades. Undeniable fun." *–NY Post.* "Joyful and unashamedly vulgar." *–The New Yorker.* "Sparkles with treasure." *–New York Sun.* [2M, 5W] ISBN: 978-0-8222-2137-1

★ **MATCH by Stephen Belber.** When a young Seattle couple meet a prominent New York choreographer, they are led on a fraught journey that will change their lives forever. "Uproariously funny, deeply moving, enthralling theatre." *–NY Daily News.* "Prolific laughs and ear-to-ear smiles." *–NY Magazine.* [2M, 1W] ISBN: 978-0-8222-2020-6

★ **MR. MARMALADE by Noah Haidle.** Four-year-old Lucy's imaginary friend, Mr. Marmalade, doesn't have much time for her—not to mention he has a cocaine addiction and a penchant for pornography. "Alternately hilarious and heartbreaking." *–The New Yorker.* "A mature and accomplished play." *–LA Times.* "Scathingly observant comedy." *–Miami Herald.* [4M, 2W] ISBN: 978-0-8222-2142-5

★ **MOONLIGHT AND MAGNOLIAS by Ron Hutchinson.** Three men cloister themselves as they work tirelessly to reshape a screenplay that's just not working—*Gone with the Wind.* "Consumers of vintage Hollywood insider stories will eat up Hutchinson's diverting conjecture." *–Variety.* "A lot of fun." *–NY Post.* "A Hollywood dream-factory farce." *–Chicago Sun-Times.* [3M, 1W] ISBN: 978-0-8222-2084-8

★ **THE LEARNED LADIES OF PARK AVENUE by David Grimm, translated and freely adapted from Molière's *Les Femmes Savantes.*** Dicky wants to marry Betty, but her mother's plan is for Betty to wed a most pompous man. "A brave, brainy and barmy revision." *–Hartford Courant.* "A rare but welcome bird in contemporary theatre." *–New Haven Register.* "Roll over Cole Porter." *–Boston Globe.* [5M, 5W] ISBN: 978-0-8222-2135-7

★ **REGRETS ONLY by Paul Rudnick.** A sparkling comedy of Manhattan manners that explores the latest topics in marriage, friendships and squandered riches. "One of the funniest quip-meisters on the planet." *–NY Times.* "Precious moments of hilarity. Devastatingly accurate political and social satire." *–BackStage.* "Great fun." *–CurtainUp.* [3M, 3W] ISBN: 978-0-8222-2223-1

NEW PLAYS

★ **AFTER ASHLEY by Gina Gionfriddo.** A teenager is unwillingly thrust into the national spotlight when a family tragedy becomes talk-show fodder. "A work that virtually any audience would find accessible." *–NY Times.* "Deft characterization and caustic humor." *–NY Sun.* "A smart satirical drama." *–Variety.* [4M, 2W] ISBN: 978-0-8222-2099-2

★ **THE RUBY SUNRISE by Rinne Groff.** Twenty-five years after Ruby struggles to realize her dream of inventing the first television, her daughter faces similar battles of faith as she works to get Ruby's story told on network TV. "Measured and intelligent, optimistic yet clear-eyed." *–NY Magazine.* "Maintains an exciting sense of ingenuity." *–Village Voice.* "Sinuous theatrical flair." *–Broadway.com.* [3M, 4W] ISBN: 978-0-8222-2140-1

★ **MY NAME IS RACHEL CORRIE taken from the writings of Rachel Corrie, edited by Alan Rickman and Katharine Viner.** This solo piece tells the story of Rachel Corrie who was killed in Gaza by an Israeli bulldozer set to demolish a Palestinian home. "Heartbreaking urgency. An invigoratingly detailed portrait of a passionate idealist." *–NY Times.* "Deeply authentically human." *–USA Today.* "A stunning dramatization." *–CurtainUp.* [1W] ISBN: 978-0-8222-2222-4

★ **ALMOST, MAINE by John Cariani.** This charming midwinter night's dream of a play turns romantic clichés on their ear as it chronicles the painfully hilarious amorous adventures (and misadventures) of residents of a remote northern town that doesn't quite exist. "A whimsical approach to the joys and perils of romance." *–NY Times.* "Sweet, poignant and witty." *–NY Daily News.* "Aims for the heart by way of the funny bone." *–Star-Ledger.* [2M, 2W] ISBN: 978-0-8222-2156-2

★ **Mitch Albom's TUESDAYS WITH MORRIE by Jeffrey Hatcher and Mitch Albom, based on the book by Mitch Albom.** The true story of Brandeis University professor Morrie Schwartz and his relationship with his student Mitch Albom. "A touching, life-affirming, deeply emotional drama." *–NY Daily News.* "You'll laugh. You'll cry." *–Variety.* "Moving and powerful." *–NY Post.* [2M] ISBN: 978-0-8222-2188-3

★ **DOG SEES GOD: CONFESSIONS OF A TEENAGE BLOCKHEAD by Bert V. Royal.** An abused pianist and a pyromaniac ex-girlfriend contribute to the teen-angst of America's most hapless kid. "A welcome antidote to the notion that the *Peanuts* gang provides merely American cuteness." *–NY Times.* "Hysterically funny." *–NY Post.* "The *Peanuts* kids have finally come out of their shells." *–Time Out.* [4M, 4W] ISBN: 978-0-8222-2152-4

NEW PLAYS

★ **RABBIT HOLE by David Lindsay-Abaire.** Winner of the 2007 Pulitzer Prize. Becca and Howie Corbett have everything a couple could want until a life-shattering accident turns their world upside down. "An intensely emotional examination of grief, laced with wit." *–Variety.* "A transcendent and deeply affecting new play." *–Entertainment Weekly.* "Painstakingly beautiful." *–BackStage.* [2M, 3W] ISBN: 978-0-8222-2154-8

★ **DOUBT, A Parable by John Patrick Shanley.** Winner of the 2005 Pulitzer Prize and Tony Award. Sister Aloysius, a Bronx school principal, takes matters into her own hands when she suspects the young Father Flynn of improper relations with one of the male students. "All the elements come invigoratingly together like clockwork." *–Variety.* "Passionate, exquisite, important, engrossing." *–NY Newsday.* [1M, 3W] ISBN: 978-0-8222-2219-4

★ **THE PILLOWMAN by Martin McDonagh.** In an unnamed totalitarian state, an author of horrific children's stories discovers that someone has been making his stories come true. "A blindingly bright black comedy." *–NY Times.* "McDonagh's least forgiving, bravest play." *–Variety.* "Thoroughly startling and genuinely intimidating." *–Chicago Tribune.* [4M, 5 bit parts (2M, 1W, 1 boy, 1 girl)] ISBN: 978-0-8222-2100-5

★ **GREY GARDENS book by Doug Wright, music by Scott Frankel, lyrics by Michael Korie.** The hilarious and heartbreaking story of Big Edie and Little Edie Bouvier Beale, the eccentric aunt and cousin of Jacqueline Kennedy Onassis, once bright names on the social register who became East Hampton's most notorious recluses. "An experience no passionate theatergoer should miss." *–NY Times.* "A unique and unmissable musical." *–Rolling Stone.* [4M, 3W, 2 girls] ISBN: 978-0-8222-2181-4

★ **THE LITTLE DOG LAUGHED by Douglas Carter Beane.** Mitchell Green could make it big as the hot new leading man in Hollywood if Diane, his agent, could just keep him in the closet. "Devastatingly funny." *–NY Times.* "An out-and-out delight." *–NY Daily News.* "Full of wit and wisdom." *–NY Post.* [2M, 2W] ISBN: 978-0-8222-2226-2

★ **SHINING CITY by Conor McPherson.** A guilt-ridden man reaches out to a therapist after seeing the ghost of his recently deceased wife. "Haunting, inspired and glorious." *–NY Times.* "Simply breathtaking and astonishing." *–Time Out.* "A thoughtful, artful, absorbing new drama." *–Star-Ledger.* [3M, 1W] ISBN: 978-0-8222-2187-6